NO OTHER DOCTRINE

NO OTHER DOCTRINE

The Gospel
and the
Postmodern World

by

John F Parkinson

JOHN RITCHIE LTD
CHRISTIAN PUBLICATIONS

40 Beansburn, Kilmarnock, Scotland

ISBN 1 904064 29 9

Copyright © 2005 by John Ritchie Ltd.
40 Beansburn, Kilmarnock, Scotland

Typeset by John Ritchie Ltd., Kilmarnock
Printed by Bell & Bain

Contents

For Andrea and Matthew

Acknowledgements

I am indebted to the following Christian friends who read the drafts and offered many valuable suggestions: Mr Walter Boyd (whose enthusiasm and constant encouragement helped me over the finishing line), Dr Robert Cargill (who has very kindly written the Foreword), Mr Leslie Craig, Mr David Gilliland, Dr David Gooding, Mr Andrew Logan, Dr Clark Logan, and Mr Paul McMullan. I wish to thank Mr Edwin Taylor and his colleagues at John Ritchie Limited for publishing the book. Thanks are also due to Mr John Grant for his interest and valued help. Finally, I gladly acknowledge the unfailing support of my family. Thank you once again, Andrea and Matthew.

Foreword

To say that we live in a changing and confused world is a classic understatement. In almost every country, the rate of change is such that people are swept along hardly knowing where they are, where they have come from, or where they are going. Opinions about origins, purpose, and destiny are more diverse than ever, more and more complex, more and more confused. Very many people are now quite unsure of what to believe, of what is real and what is fantasy, of what is truth and what is imagination.

In the privileged situation of the UK (or any other developed country), isn't it strange that after a century and a half of unrestricted education, clear answers are not available, especially to questions about what is right and wrong, true and false, good and bad? The pioneers of the educational movement in the nineteenth century had no doubts about these matters. One of the main reasons for establishing schools in every community was to promote Biblical knowledge, and stabilise, even advance society, upon the firm foundations of the Ten Commandments.

What has happened now? The whole thing has been turned around. In the last fifty years or so, those very institutions which had their roots in Christianity, have spearheaded doubts about God, with a new agenda promoting atheism and its allied beliefs. Sad to say the god of this age has exploited this to blind the minds of especially young people, lest the light of the Gospel of Christ should shine in. In place of honest questions of enquiry have come loaded questions with ulterior motives. The Dark Ages were superseded by the Reformation with its well known quotation, "The just shall live by faith". Then the Renaissance led to the Enlightenment with the dictum, "Intellect and Reason will Guide". We have now come through Modernism to Postmodernism where we are told that there are no rules or reasons for anything!

In this twenty first century, more information than ever is available, more research is done in every field, but certainty and assurance have become elusive. With time honoured institutions discarded, foundations eroded, light refused, distinctions blurred, social fabric in tatters, is there nothing of enduring value, of certainty and truth? Is there no solid rock to build on? No anchor which will hold when the cross winds of opinion blow fiercely, when the shock waves of politically correct but morally corrupt pronouncements assail?

There is. "THE WORD OF THE LORD ENDURETH FOR EVER." What a contrast to man's knowledge, its glory as fickle and failing as the yellowing grass in an autumn field! Our Lord said, "Heaven and earth shall pass away: but My words shall not pass away." (Mark 13:31)

The book you have in your hands is based upon the Word of the Lord. That is why it is entitled "No Other Doctrine". It will show you the origin and the outcome of theories which abandon this divine revelation. From the dogmatism of evolution theory has emerged the relativism of any theory you want, and eventually the illogical position that there is no meaning in anything anyway. It's all in the mind, or it is socially determined or linguistically constructed. Believe whatever suits you!

You could be excused for now saying, "And what does all that mean?", because a system of belief without secure foundations is meaningless, no matter what fine words dress it up. In the same way, a life without the knowledge of God through Jesus Christ whom He sent is profitless, no matter what fine achievements fill it up.

Man's problem is not ignorance of what is demonstrably true, but rejection of what is practically undesirable by those for whom facing up to the truth would demand a change they are unwilling to make. Our Lord Himself said of them, "Light is come into the world, and men loved darkness rather than light, because their deeds were evil" (John 3:19). He said also, "I am the Light of the world. He that follows Me shall not walk in darkness but shall have the light of life" (John 8.12). Countless thousands have discovered the truth in these words, and have found the life in His light. In John 14:6 are His unambiguous words: "I am the way, the truth, and the life: no one comes to the Father but by Me". Attempts to modify this fundamental statement of the Christian gospel and make it more acceptable to modern or postmodern man are doomed to fail. It cannot be changed. If it were, it would be no more reliable than any other message or theory which has had to be modified and changed before being abandoned to the dustbin of history. There is no other doctrine.

The author of this book has done his research thoroughly and written it clearly, and I recommend that you read it all. Young people exposed to current ideas in their education, older people who should try to understand how society is changing, and honest but confused seekers after truth will all benefit from these pages. Early chapters contain a detailed account of the doctrine of the gospel which has never changed, followed by a description of the often hostile reception this gospel received from different first century audiences. Later chapters describe recent and current theories which will soon change to be replaced by others, all of them anticipated in the pages of your Bible. They originate from the "father of lies" who in every possible way tries to close hearts to the consistent call of Christ in the gospel: "Come unto Me, all ye that labour and are heavy laden, and I will give you rest" (Mat 11.28).

There is one other important reason for this book. It is to give a fresh incentive for us to proclaim the gospel to a people who need it more than ever. This gospel must be Bible based and Christ centred, as it was in the days of the Acts of the Apostles. It must be founded upon the death, burial, and resurrection of Jesus Christ, the Son of God. There is "another gospel" (Gal 1:6-7), a perverted one which is not Bible based and not Christ centred. Those who preach such a false gospel, man made and fundamentally flawed, receive the strongest of censures (v. 8-9). It was around in the first century, and persists today for example among those who would tell us that ecumenism is the way forward.

Those who do proclaim the true gospel must do so with unambiguous loyalty to its Author and its Subject. They also require to be aware of the background beliefs of their audience, who, as shown in the following chapters, are now very confused and ignorant of spiritual matters. They will make the gospel known with the clear conviction that only "Christ crucified" can meet man's deepest need. May you be, or become, one of those who carry such convictions, and find them strengthened by the reading of, and repeated reference to, the pages which follow.

Bert Cargill
St Monans,
Scotland
May 2005

Introduction

"Pilate saith unto him, What is truth?" (John 18:38)

Let us, for a moment, imagine that we are in a room with three different kinds of thinkers: a Christian, a modernist and a postmodernist. We are going to ask each one in turn a question about the nature of knowledge: *Can we know for certain the truth and reality behind this universe?*

The Christian, answering first, responds with a resounding 'yes'. The reality behind all created things is God, and God has made Himself known in the Bible. For the Christian, the truth behind the universe can most certainly be known, because it has been revealed.

On turning to the modernist, with his Enlightenment mindset, we hear a different kind of answer. We can know things for certain, confirms the modernist, although such knowledge does not come from God or from the Bible, but comes from unaided human reason. Scientific enquiry and human progress shall one day arrive at the truth behind our existence. Such is the view of the modernist.

Finally, we ask the postmodern thinker whether or not we can know anything for certain. It is illusory to speak of discovering truth by human reason, he says, because there is no such thing as truth to be discovered. We cannot know anything for certain, because there is nothing to know. All truth, value and meaning are merely man-made constructions. Our postmodern friend assures us that truth is relative rather than absolute. In other words, what is true for you might not be true for me. We simply create our own ideas of truth according to our culture and language. No belief system can claim to be true in any exclusive sense. Further, there are no moral absolutes to govern human behaviour. Everything, including the concept of right and wrong, is socially determined There is no ultimate meaning to life and no truth behind the universe. Such is the thinking of today's postmodernism.

For the reader who is not familiar with the terminology, we can summarise this introductory soundbite by noting that the three different approaches to knowledge are based on *revelation*, *reason* and *relativism*:

- Christianity is founded on the actuality of divine *revelation*.
- Modernism is a philosophical outlook which enthrones human *reason*.
- Postmodernism is the more recent philosophical trend which sees everything in terms of *relativism*.

What is the truth and reality behind the universe and human life? The Bible gives us the only certain answer, "In the beginning God created the heaven and the earth" (Gen 1:1). Christians regard this statement as true in the absolute, universal, objective and eternal sense. No Christian would entertain the thought that this statement might be true for some, but not for others. Indeed, such a proposition would rightly be regarded as inconsistent with common sense. The statement affirming God as the Creator of all things is true in the absolute sense, transcending all boundaries of time and culture. It is true in the universal sense, whether we are European, American, Asian, African or Australian. It is true in the objective sense, regardless of whether we believe it or not. It is true in the eternal sense, in that it will never be invalidated in time or eternity. It is this certain knowledge that gives purpose, value, and meaning to human life.

In recent times, the western world has experienced a seismic shift of attitude in the spheres of philosophy, religion, politics and education. Past generations had no difficulty in thinking in terms of moral absolutes and objective truth. But the new generation of thinkers has abandoned such concepts as outmoded, preferring to think in terms of relativism, pluralism and subjective truth. We are now being told that there is no such thing as objective truth that might be universally applicable to all men at all times. In other words, what is true for one person may be false for another.

What is postmodernism? As a working definition, postmodernism can be regarded as a philosophical and cultural movement of the late twentieth century which rejects the concept of absolute truth, insisting that all such notions are relative and rooted in culture. Postmodernism is therefore a creed of relativism.

What are the implications of this view for the Christian gospel? Christianity is dismissed as a mere social construct, the product of a particular view of culture and language. Postmodernism is the rejection of absolute truth and of human significance, claiming that truth is relative rather than absolute; temporal rather than eternal; ethnic rather than universal; pluralist rather than exclusive; fragmented rather than unified. The postmodern agenda strikes at the foundations of Christian doctrine and the truth revealed in the Bible.

The message of modernism, which came out of eighteenth century Enlightenment humanism, was that truth could be discovered by human reason. The new message of postmodernism is that there is actually no such thing as truth to be discovered. Modernism rejected the revealed truth of the Bible in favour of human reason. Postmodernism has gone further and has abandoned the assumptions of modernism in favour of relativism. Postmodernism, therefore, is a philosophical outlook resulting from the collapse of confidence in the old certainties and assumptions of the Enlightenment. This paradigm shift in thinking has been enthusiastically adopted by the universities, the media, and even the churches. It is reshaping society's ideas about truth, behaviour, responsibility, value, and purpose. We shall presently consider these issues in greater detail.

Why have I written this book, and who will benefit from it? Firstly, this book is written to help, at an introductory level, college and university students who will come up against the influences of the postmodern outlook in the course of their studies. Secondly, it is written to alert an older generation of preachers, teachers, and parents, who have a desire, if only for their children's sake, to be aware of these things. And thirdly, I also pray that some non-Christians will read the book, and that God might be pleased to use it to bring some such readers to "the knowledge of the truth" (1 Tim 2:4).

But first, I must declare my interests! I freely acknowledge that I have not written this book as an impartial observer, but from a Christian point of view. I make no apology for that. I am glad to be a Christian. Nevertheless, we shall see that postmodernism is not only anti-Christian, but is also sheer nonsense from a philosophical point of view.

What then are the implications of this postmodern way of thinking for the preaching of the gospel? Paradoxically the new movement, which claims to be tolerant toward all the religious systems of the world, is totally intolerant of the exclusive claims of Christianity. However, this is no new phenomenon. The gospel of Jesus Christ was originally preached in the ancient world against a background of Judaism and Paganism, and it met with extreme hostility and intolerance from both camps. Many of the objections and arguments with which the early church had to contend have resurfaced in our own age. In this book, we propose to take a considered look at the problems facing gospel preachers in New Testament times, and so equip ourselves better to proclaim the gospel to our own impoverished generation.

The first century world was turned upside down by a radically new message. A tiny insignificant group of disciples at Jerusalem had been preaching and teaching that salvation was to be found in a Person. They were boldly proclaiming that Jesus of Nazareth, whom the Jewish and Roman authorities had judicially murdered, was the long-awaited Messiah of Israel and the Saviour of the world.

At the beginning, the new converts were almost exclusively Jewish and confined to Jerusalem. They met in the temple daily and practised what was nothing less than a prototype pattern for every future local church - they received the Word, were baptised, and continued steadfastly in the apostles' doctrine, fellowship, in breaking of bread and in prayers (Acts 2:41-42). On the day of Pentecost three thousand converts were added to their number.

Quickly the 'movement' spread throughout Judea. Then reports came to the church at Jerusalem that Samaritans too were believing. Philip had gone to a city of Samaria and "preached Christ unto them" (Acts 8:5). The gospel met with a remarkable response and the people with one accord gave heed to Philip's message. When news of the Samaritan conversions reached the ears of the apostles in Jerusalem, they sent Peter and John to help them. The Samaritan believers, who had been baptised in the name of the Lord Jesus, did not receive the Holy Spirit until the apostles from Jerusalem had laid their hands on them, thus confirming the truth of the Lord's words to the woman of Samaria, "Salvation is of the Jews" (John 4:22). While returning to Jerusalem, Peter and John preached the gospel in many Samaritan villages.

Then the most startling news of all began to filter through to the church at Jerusalem. It was reported that in the Syrian city of Antioch even Gentiles were turning to the Lord. It was difficult enough for Jewish believers to accept that God had brought Samaritans into gospel blessing, but it was nothing less than incredible that pagan Gentiles should also be included! Once again, the Jerusalem church wanted to check out the reports and to assess the situation. The man chosen for the task on that occasion was Barnabas, described as "a good man and full of the Holy Ghost and of faith" (Acts 11:24). On his arrival at Antioch, Barnabas saw the grace of God and was glad. He exhorted the Gentile believers that with purpose of heart they would cleave to the Lord. Barnabas then went on a 'search and find' mission to the city of Tarsus in Cilicia, looking for Saul of Tarsus to share in the teaching and preaching ministry at Antioch. On finding Saul, he brought him to Antioch where they both remained and helped the church for a whole year. The assembly of believers at Antioch became the first truly "Gentile" church, and it was there that the disciples were first called Christians.

The church at Antioch subsequently commended Saul and Barnabas to go and preach the gospel in other lands. And so started the famous missionary journeys that would have such far-reaching implications for the whole world. Saul, or rather Paul as he came to be known, adopted a standard procedure as he approached each new town and city with the gospel. First, he would go to the local synagogue, if one existed, and preach the gospel to the Jews. Second, after giving the Jews every opportunity to repent, he would preach the gospel to the Gentiles. But as the Jews persistently rejected the gospel message, Paul turned more and more to the Gentiles, until at the close of the Acts of the Apostles, we read Paul's words to the Jews in Rome "Be it known therefore unto you, that the salvation of God is sent unto the Gentiles, and that they will hear it" (Acts 28:28).

The flow of gospel blessing had spread out from Jerusalem and Judea, to Samaria and eventually to the whole world. This was exactly as the Lord Jesus had said to the apostles immediately prior to His ascension - "and ye shall be witnesses unto me both in Jerusalem, and in all Judea, and in Samaria, and unto the uttermost part of the earth" (Acts 1:8).

What kind of reception did the preaching of the gospel normally receive? Was it all plain sailing or was there opposition? How did the various civil and religious authorities in each city and region respond to the gospel? We know from the Acts of the Apostles that there was a very deep and sustained opposition to the new message. Whatever it was that Paul was preaching, it was perceived as a dangerous threat to the old certainties, beliefs and customs. Both Jews and Gentiles reacted with riots, imprisonments, scourgings and persecutions. But in addition to opposition in the form of physical violence and naked aggression, there were also serious religious, political and philosophical objections raised against the truth of the gospel. Paul not only *preached* the gospel, but also often found himself having to *defend* the gospel. When the truth of the gospel was at stake, Paul was prepared to answer and refute any attacks, whether from Jewish objectors or Greek philosophers. In fact, on occasions he found himself in prison for that very thing. When in a Roman jail, Paul wrote to the believers in Philippi to tell them how much he appreciated their support, "...I have you in my heart; inasmuch as both in my bonds, and in the defence and confirmation of the gospel, ye all are partakers of my grace" (Phil 1:7).

The word 'defence' is a translation of the Greek *apologia*, from which comes the English word 'apologetics'. It is the premise of this book that Christians ought to be able, not only to preach the gospel, but also to *defend* the gospel in the twenty-first century. The gospel is under attack today from postmodern philosophy and New Age mysticism. For the sake of our children we must be able to both preach and defend the gospel.

The first century objections to the gospel came from both Jews and Gentiles. In mainstream Judaism there was a general revulsion at the thought of the crucified Jesus of Nazareth being the Christ. A very major part of Paul's ministry was to show that the One who suffered was their Messiah, and that it was *necessary* that He should have thus suffered. Then there were Jews who had professed faith in Christ, but felt it was necessary to retain the law of Moses. Some went further and demanded that Gentile believers also ought to keep the law of Moses, and that they could not be saved unless they did so. In the Gentile world Paul came up against the ideas and practices of Greek philosophy, idolatry, and sheer hedonism. Many of the new converts would have had a Greek mindset. Paul would need to preach and teach the whole counsel of God to those who had previously been idolaters.

Paul summed up the two prevailing attitudes in his letter to the church at Corinth: "But we preach Christ crucified, unto the Jews a stumbling block, and unto the Greeks foolishness" (1 Cor 1:23). The purpose of this book is that together we might take a journey into the times of Paul to observe how he handled the problems and objections that hindered the gospel in the first century world. We shall then come forward to our own times and see if our findings are of any value in addressing some twenty-first century objections to the gospel. We shall discover that the Bible is absolutely up-to-date and is all we need when we are required to defend the truth of the gospel to our own generation.

Before we consider and compare the spiritual viruses of the first and the twenty-first centuries, it will be necessary to remind ourselves concerning the content of the gospel message as originally proclaimed by the apostles. That is the aim of Chapter 1. In Chapters 2 and 3 we examine the response of the ancient world to the gospel of Christ. The subject of Chapter 4 is the impact on the gospel of the modern, rationalistic age, which started with the eighteenth century Enlightenment, and lasted through to the late 1900s. In Chapter 5 we take a fresh look at the important question of origins. In Chapter 6, we consider the implications of postmodernity for the gospel. We shall see that both twenty-first century postmodern philosophy and New Age mysticism are remarkably similar to the Epicureanism and Stoicism that Paul encountered in Athens, recorded for us in Acts 17.

It is at this point that I can imagine some readers, especially older ones, claiming that they really do not need to know about postmodernism, and that they will carry on preaching the same gospel regardless of prevailing philosophies. In a certain sense I have much sympathy with this view. It is indeed vital to go on preaching the same gospel, and that is the standpoint of this book. However, it is also vital to understand that our young people are being educated in the language, premises and terminology of postmodern philosophy. Ought we not as parents to be interested in what our families may be imbibing at school and university? This is nothing less than a debate about the very nature of knowledge and truth. I suggest that we should and must familiarise ourselves with what our children are being taught. We who are older owe it to the younger generation to teach them the truth and to warn them of error, and to hand on a pure and scriptural gospel. Let us endeavour to be like the men of Issachar, who were described as "men that had *understanding of the times*, to know what Israel ought to do" (1 Chron 12:32).

May God be pleased to bless this book to those readers, both younger and older, who wish to have a more scriptural understanding of the times in which we live.

CHAPTER 1

The Gospel that Paul Preached

Many people believe and teach that the gospel is a code of ethics, simply a matter of doing one's best. Those who think in such terms invariably point to the Sermon on the Mount as the essential content of the gospel. And increasingly, such people believe that the gospel is not true in any exclusive sense, but is merely true in the same sense that all other belief systems are true.

Is this a valid point of view? What exactly is the message of the gospel, and does it really matter? It certainly mattered to Paul, who summarised the central truth of the gospel when writing to the church in Corinth:

"For the Jews require a sign, and the Greeks seek after wisdom: but we preach *Christ crucified*, unto the Jews a stumbling block, and unto the Greeks foolishness; but unto them which are called, both Jews and Greeks, Christ the power of God, and the wisdom of God" (1 Cor 1:22-24).

No man has ever suffered more for the gospel than the apostle Paul. He endured imprisonments, countless beatings, and was often close to death. Five times he received from the Jews the customary forty lashes save one, something hardly imaginable in modern times. He was beaten with rods three times and was stoned at least once. He was shipwrecked on at least three occasions. He frequently experienced the hazards of travel in the ancient world and was in constant danger from both rivers and robbers. His own people, as well as the Gentiles, meant him harm. He was safe in neither city nor desert, and suffered the privations of weariness, hardship, sleepless nights, hunger, thirst, cold and exposure - all for the sake of the gospel.

Why did Paul experience such hostility from both Jews and Gentiles? Why was he in prison? Could he have avoided incarceration by simply modifying the gospel message in some small way? Would it have been possible to make the gospel less offensive to the Jews and to the Roman authorities? Before we can address such questions, we must clearly understand the essential content of the gospel. For Paul, the gospel was non-negotiable, and he was unwilling to compromise its truth.

When Paul wrote his famous epistle to the Romans, he went to great lengths to explain and expound the gospel. He accomplished this by portraying a courtroom scene to which a first century Roman could readily relate. Happily, for us in the twenty-first century, the illustration is still as relevant and helpful as it was in Paul's time. We are all familiar with a court system that has a judge and defendant, prosecution and defence, with resulting verdict and sentence. Let us, as it were, step inside this courtroom scene and follow the proceedings. It is of immense importance that we do so, for it is you and I who are in the dock.

THE JUDGE

Who is the Judge? This is a critical question, seeing that the ruling of the court will derive its authority from the Judge. We are left in no doubt as to the identity of the Judge - He is God. There can be no higher court, there can be no greater justice, and there can be no further appeal. This is the Creator calling His creatures to give account. We are not speaking of God as a kind of universal energy or impersonal force. We are speaking of the infinite personal God of the Bible. He alone has the right to judge His creation. His verdict will be sovereign and final. However, as we shall see, He is also the God and Father of our Lord Jesus Christ. That will be good news for the accused in the dock.

THE ACCUSED

The hard truth is that you and I are in the dock. It is the whole world, all mankind, which is being charged. That makes it very important that we pay close attention to the proceedings, because we are going to learn God's estimate of each one of us. It will not be complimentary - it will severely damage our pride. As we stand in the dock, we must listen to the charges being read out. The list is long and the charges are very serious. In fact, every charge is a capital offence.

THE CHARGES

The first accusation that Paul brings against mankind is that they had become *perverse in their thinking*. As men surveyed the visible wonders of creation, it should have been clearly evident to them that these things had a Creator. What can be known about God is plain to men, because God has shown it to them. God's eternal power and deity are clearly perceived in the things that have been made. So much so, says Paul, that "they are without excuse" (Rom 1:20). Instead of acknowledging God as the Creator, they refused to give Him glory or thanks. So what did they do? They made images of men, birds, animals and reptiles and gave the glory to them. Paul wrote, "Professing themselves to be wise, they became fools..." (Rom 1:22). In their minds, men exchanged the truth about God for a lie and worshipped the creation rather than the Creator. In their religious thinking, men had become fools. It was not that men were fools in the sense of lacking intelligence, but that they were fools because of their wilful rejection of plain truth.

Men have still not changed since Paul penned those words. The world of modern science, the press and media, all do their best to explain away the idea of God. They certainly have no time for the living God of the Bible. Men are still futile and vain in their thinking, and their senseless minds are still darkened. In our own day, men are again worshipping the creation more than the Creator. Professing to be wise, they are more foolish than ever. Therefore, the first charge is that men have become perverse in their thinking.

The second major charge is that consequently men had become *perverse in their conduct*. God allowed man's foolish thinking to take its course until his very behaviour was corrupted. Paul put it in these words: "Wherefore God also gave them up to uncleanness through the lusts of their own hearts, to dishonour their own bodies between themselves: who changed the truth of God into a lie, and worshipped and served the creature more than the Creator, who is blessed forever. Amen." (Rom 1:24-25).

Men and women began to violate the laws of nature. Forsaking the natural and creatorial order of marriage between male and female, they preferred unnatural physical relations between people of the same sex. Paul variously describes this kind of misconduct as unclean, dishonouring, vile and unseemly. It was not simply that such things are unnatural, but that they are *against* nature. The idea of men with men, and women with women, is a violation of nature.

It is important to note that this type of gross behaviour was what characterised the cities of Sodom and Gomorrah. Abraham's nephew Lot was an inhabitant of Sodom and barely escaped its judgement. The Lord Jesus warned the men of His day that, just as it had been in the days of Lot, so "shall it be in the day when the Son of man is revealed" (Luke 17:28-30). How are we to understand the Lord's prediction? It means simply that at the time of the second coming of Christ history will have turned full circle and the world will once again be characterised by the very sin that is forever associated with Sodom. We leave it to the reader to decide how close we must be to the Lord's return.

Just as men did not see fit to acknowledge God, so God abandoned them to a base mind and to improper conduct. As if the charges of perverseness in thinking and conduct were not enough, Paul continues with a formidable list of sins:

"unrighteousness, fornication, wickedness, covetousness, malice, envy, murder, strife, deceit, malignity, gossip, slander, haters of God, despiteful, proud, boasters, inventors of evil things, disobedient to parents, foolish, covenant breakers, heartless, ruthless" (Rom 1:29-31).

To make matters worse, Paul observes that the men who do

such things are well aware of God's judgement. In fact, not only do they know that those who do such things deserve to die, but they actually approve those who practise them. Things are now looking very bad for mankind, for you and me. It is not that every person has committed each sin mentioned (although the potential for every sin is in us all), but the charge is that "all have sinned and come short of the glory of God" (Rom 3:23). According to these charges, we all have true moral guilt before God.

Unfortunately, Paul is not finished with us yet, for there is worse to come. Not only are we *guilty* sinners but we shall now be shown to be *ruined* sinners. That is to say, there is absolutely no possibility of self-recovery. Man cannot 'undo' the sins he has committed, nor can he deliver himself from committing them. His very nature is fallen, sinful and ruined. Every part of the human personality has been contaminated by sin. There is nothing of self which man can offer to God that would be acceptable to Him. Paul describes man's ruined condition in the following graphic terms: "Their *throat* is an open sepulchre; with their *tongues* they have used deceit; the poison of asps is under their *lips*: whose *mouth* is full of cursing and bitterness: their *feet* are swift to shed blood: destruction and misery are in their ways: and the way of peace have they not known: there is no fear of God before their *eyes*." (Rom 3:13-18). Paul informs us that all of man has been spoiled by sin, hence the references to the throat, the tongue, the lips, the mouth, the feet and the eyes.

Therefore, the charge is that all men are guilty, ruined sinners. To prove his case, Paul is now going to call two witnesses against us.

WITNESSES AGAINST THE ACCUSED

The first witness against mankind is **the law of Moses**. God chose the nation of Israel to make Himself known in a very special way. The Jewish people received a law-code which established an absolute standard of conduct that God required of them. God had acquainted the people with the concept of sin. They fully understood that there was a total prohibition on such things as stealing, killing, adultery, lying and coveting. However, instead of delivering the people from sinning, the law simply pointed the finger at them and condemned them. The law exposed the inherent inability of man to live without sinning. It was not that the Jews were worse than the Gentiles, but simply that they were a representative sample of all men. The German writer Erich Sauer has helpfully said: "Israel's course is an instructive object lesson, given on the open stage of world history, a warning example for all nations, a mirror for every individual."[1] The law of Moses, therefore, bears witness to the charge that men are guilty, ruined, sinners.

However, someone may well ask - How about people on the other side of the world who have never heard of the law of Moses? They do not know that God has prohibited these things, nor do they understand the concept of sin. Can you really call such people guilty sinners?

Now Paul calls his second witness, *human conscience*. When a man on the other side of the world goes to steal from his neighbour, he experiences an inner conviction that his action is wrong and that he ought not to be doing such a thing. The man may have no knowledge of the law of Moses and yet he has an instinctive sense of right and wrong. Where did he get the idea that stealing was wrong? It is of course the man's conscience that is accusing him. His conscience tells him that such things as stealing, killing, adultery and lying are wrong. Paul says that when Gentiles who have not the law do by nature what the law requires, they are a law unto themselves, even though they do not have the law. It will be their conscience that will accuse or perhaps excuse them on that day when God will judge the secrets of men by Jesus Christ. The moral sense of right and wrong points to God as the basis for such morality. So human conscience also witnesses against man that he is a guilty sinner.

Paul informs us that "as many as have sinned without law

---

[1] Sauer, Erich *The Dawn of World Redemption* (Paternoster Press, 1977) p.151.

shall also perish without law: and as many as have sinned in the law shall be judged by the law" (see Rom 2:11-16). In other words, the *law* will witness against the Jews that they are sinners, while *conscience* will witness against the Gentiles that they too are sinners.

The case for the prosecution, so to speak, now rests. The charges have been catalogued and the witnesses have been called. The world now stands accused before God and the case against us is summed up in the terse words of Romans 3:23 "For all have sinned, and come short of the glory of God."

THE DEFENCE

As in every proper court of law, there is an opportunity for the accused to present their defence. However, on this occasion Paul informs us that every mouth is *stopped* (Rom 3:19). It is not that God will not allow man to say anything, but rather that man has nothing to say. He has heard the charges and he is totally silent. Men are entirely without excuse. No defence is offered.

WITNESSES FOR THE DEFENCE

No witnesses are called to the defence of mankind. The whole world, you and I included, must stand in silence and await the verdict of the living God.

THE VERDICT

The solemn words are pronounced - "All the world...*guilty* before God" (Rom 3:19). God has ruled that the charges against us are true and accurate. The case is proven - men are guilty, ruined sinners. Nothing remains for us but to await the sentence.

THE SENTENCE

Every single sin is a capital offence and carries the sentence of death. Paul tells us that "the wages of sin is *death*" (Rom 6:23). If we die in our sins, we shall be eternally separated from God. It is in the book of Revelation where we learn that death and hell will one day be cast into the lake of fire (Rev 20:14). However, the sentence of God has already been pronounced against us. John tells us that "he that believeth not is condemned *already*" (John 3:18). So not only are we guilty, ruined sinners, but we now discover that we are also *condemned* sinners. The proceedings have been painful. We have been stripped of every ounce of pride. The charges are true and our mouths are stopped. The truth of the matter is that we are guilty, ruined and condemned.

INTERLUDE

Gospel preachers sometimes speak of the gospel in terms of *man's ruin* and *God's remedy*. So far, we have concentrated on man's ruin; now we will focus on God's remedy, for happily God has provided a way whereby guilty, ruined, condemned sinners can be made right with Him. This brings us to the heart of the gospel.

THE OFFERED PARDON

How can God offer pardon to condemned men and women without compromising His own standards of justice? Can God forgive guilty sinners on a righteous basis? The answer to the question is YES because *the sentence of the court has been transferred to another.* There was One who was able and willing to take the guilty sinner's place and to die for him, even as him. We are ungodly sinners who have no strength to remedy our condition before God, but Paul's words bring the best news we could ever hear: "For when we were yet without strength, in due time *Christ died for the ungodly*" (Rom 5:6).

The good news is that God sent His Son to be the Saviour of the world. The Son of God came down from heaven and entered humanity. For the first time in the history of this world, there was a man who kept the law of Moses in its totality and never once offended His conscience in any matter. In fact, Paul tells us that the Lord Jesus "knew no sin" (2 Cor 5:21); Peter says that He "did no sin" (1 Pet 2:22); and John affirms that "in Him is no sin" (1 John 3:5). Sin was absolutely foreign to his nature, and there was nothing in Him to respond to sin. The Bible teaches very clearly both the deity and the holy humanity of the Lord Jesus Christ.

So how was the sentence of the court transferred to Christ? For the answer to the question, we must turn to the cross of Calvary. It was on the cross that the transaction took place. It was there that "Christ died for our sins" (1 Cor 15:3). Apart from His death there could be no pardon - it was really 'our death' that He died. Why should God give His Son to suffer and die for rebel sinners? Paul informs us of the Divine motive: "For God commendeth *his love* toward us, in that, while we were yet sinners, Christ died for us" (Rom 5:8).

God displayed His complete satisfaction with what His Son had accomplished by raising Him from the dead. The cross has now provided a righteous basis for God to forgive sinners. In fact, the sinner can now be made right with God, and declared righteous. Because of Calvary, God can now deal with the whole world in grace. Judgment is on hold while grace reigns. Paul describes the blessings that now flow from the throne of God toward guilty sinners: "For as by one man's disobedience many were made sinners, so by the obedience of one shall many be made righteous. Moreover the law entered, that the offence might abound. But where sin abounded, grace did much more abound: that as sin reigned unto death, *even so might grace reign* through righteousness unto eternal life by Jesus Christ our Lord" (Rom 5:19-21).

However, if judgment has been put on hold, and God is dealing with the world in grace, how do I personally come into the good of God's grace? In other words, what must I do to be saved? Happily the answer to this vital question brings salvation within the reach of all. Paul says that because of Calvary, God is just and "the justifier of him which believeth in Jesus" (Rom 3:26). That is the simplest definition of a Christian in our Bible - *"one who believes in Jesus"*. Salvation is through faith in the Lord Jesus Christ, and by 'faith' we simply mean resting on what God has said and on what Christ has done. God provides salvation by His grace, and the sinner receives it by his faith. The sinner cannot contribute one iota to his or her salvation. It is not by works, it is the gift of God.

Sinners do not put God in their debt, nor do they negotiate with God in the matter of their salvation. If guilty men are to be saved, it will be entirely on God's initiative and by His prerogative. As Paul said to the believers in Ephesus "For by grace are ye saved through faith; and that not of yourselves: it is the gift of God: not of works, lest any man should boast" (Eph 2:8-9).

Because salvation is by simple, personal faith in Christ, it is brought within the reach of the old and young, the rich and poor, the black and white, the Jew and the Gentile. All must come on the same terms. There is no advantage for the Jew and no disadvantage for the Gentile. Paul asked, "Is he the God of the Jews only? is he not also of the Gentiles? Yes, of the Gentiles also: seeing it is one God, which shall justify the circumcision (Jews) by faith, and uncircumcision (Gentiles) through faith" (Rom 3:29-30). One way, and only one way, has been opened for all. There is no other way to come.

HEIRS OF GOD

When a condemned sinner comes to Christ and trusts Him for salvation, how does that affect his or her standing with God? Paul informs us "Therefore being justified by faith, we have peace with God through our Lord Jesus Christ" (Rom 5:1). Every single sin has been forgiven, and the cause of enmity has been removed. The moment that a person places his faith in Christ, God reckons the death of Christ to him. That is to say, when I trusted Christ as my Saviour, I came into all the good of what Christ had done for me. My very status and standing with God changed radically. In fact, God now sees me "in Christ". From having been a condemned sinner, the believer is now delivered and saved from the penalty of sin: "There is therefore now no condemnation to them which are in Christ Jesus" (Rom 8:1). The legal status of 'condemned' has been changed to the legal status of 'justified', i.e. declared righteous. God is satisfied that the penalty for my sins has been fully discharged in the death of Christ. I will never be charged with those sins again. In fact, God now looks on that old person I was before conversion as *judicially dead*. I died with Christ, a fact that was symbolised in my baptism (Rom 6:3-4). However, if I have died with Him, I have also been raised to newness of life in Him. The believer is exhorted to consider that he is dead to sin and alive to God through Jesus Christ our Lord. The members of our body, which we once used as instruments of unrighteousness, are now to be yielded as instruments of righteousness (Rom 6:13).

The question might well be asked - how does the believer obtain the power to walk in this newness of life? After all, it has been established that not only is man a guilty sinner, he is also a *ruined* sinner. He cannot live for God on his own strength. What is the solution to this problem? Paul poses the problem like this: "For I delight in the law of God in the inward man: but I see another law in my members, warring against the law of my mind, and bringing me into captivity to the law of sin which is in my members. O wretched man that I am! who shall deliver me from the body of this death?" (Rom 7:22-24). Happily, Paul quickly provides the answer. It is through our Lord Jesus Christ and the power that He provides: "For the law of the Spirit of life in Christ Jesus hath made me free from the law of sin and death" (Rom 8:2). By the power of the indwelling Holy Spirit, the believer can live a life of victory in exactly the same body in which he was once enslaved to sin.

So not only is the Christian saved from the *penalty* of sin, but he is saved from the *power* of sin. In eternity, he will also be saved from the very *presence* of sin. Described as heirs of God and joint heirs with Christ, all believers will enjoy that great crowning purpose of God for us when we shall be "conformed to the image of his Son" (Rom 8:17,29). Can our status as 'justified' ever be reversed in this life or the next? Lest there should be any doubt, Paul tells us that neither tribulation, nor distress, nor persecution, nor famine, nor nakedness, nor peril, nor sword, nor death, nor life, nor angels, nor principalities, nor powers, nor things present, nor things to come, nor anything else in all creation, "shall be able to separate us from the love of God, which is in Christ Jesus our Lord" (Rom 8:35-39).

THE SCOPE
We have surveyed the vast scheme of salvation, largely

through the eyes of Paul as expounded by him in the first eight chapters of Romans. Far from teaching that man is inherently good, Paul has proven that man is guilty and ruined. In other words, he is a sinner by nature. He was born that way. Thankfully, however, Christ Jesus came into the world to save sinners (1 Tim 1:15). Because of Calvary, God has announced a great amnesty, as it were, to the whole world. On the ground of grace, God offers pardon and forgiveness to all. The Bible word for this great amnesty is the *gospel*, meaning "good news". Paul says that the gospel "is the power of God unto salvation to everyone that believeth" (Rom 1:16). The risen Lord commanded His disciples to preach the gospel to every creature. God wants everyone to know about His Son, and the provision that He has made on Calvary for all.

Perhaps there is an interested person reading these lines who knows nothing about this personal salvation of which we have been speaking. We can tell you with all the authority of Scripture that it is God's will for you that you might be saved. Do not let your moment of opportunity pass you by. The truth of the great gospel invitation is expressed in the beautiful words of John 3:16 "For God so loved the world, that he gave his only begotten Son, that whosoever believeth in him should not perish, but have everlasting life."

THE RESPONSE

In conclusion, the gospel tells us how guilty, ruined sinners can be forgiven, saved, and made right with God. It tells of a Saviour who died for our sins and rose again. Such was the gospel that Paul preached. The response to the message in the ancient world was two-fold, just as it is in today's world: "And some believed the things which were spoken, and some believed not" (Acts 28:24). When Paul preached in the leading cities of Jerusalem, Ephesus, Corinth, Athens and Rome, he also met with bitter opposition to these words of pardon and peace through faith in Christ. In the following chapters, we shall consider these objections in some detail.

CHAPTER 2

The Response of the Jewish World

The idea of a crucified Messiah appalled the Jews. Indeed, the bitterest opposition to the gospel came, not from the Gentiles, but from the camp of Judaism. What was the particular aspect of the gospel message that caused such offence to the Jews? Paul identified the problem exactly when he informed the Corinthians that "the Jews require a sign, and the Greeks seek after wisdom: but we preach *Christ crucified*, unto the Jews a stumblingblock, and unto the Greeks foolishness" (1 Cor 1:22-23). There were clearly two different attitudes and mindsets. Paul made a distinction between the Jewish and Gentile responses. For purposes of clarity, we can do no better than to follow Paul's own example, and consider the response of the ancient world in two parts. In this chapter, we shall look at the response of the Jews to the claims of the gospel. In the next chapter, we shall examine how the wider Gentile world reacted to the message.

The Lord Jesus had lived in the town of Nazareth until, at about thirty years of age, He commenced His public ministry. When the common people heard His words and saw His works, they responded variously - they were astonished at His doctrine (Mk 1:22); they were amazed (Mk 1:27); they were afraid (Mk 5:15); they marvelled (Mk 5:20); they were astonished with a great astonishment (Mk 5:42); they were beyond measure astonished (Mk 7:37); they were greatly amazed (Mk 9:15).

However, the Lord's humble origins would soon become an object of derision and contempt for the Jews. Even Nathanael had expressed his disdain with the question "Can there any good thing come out of Nazareth?" (John 1:46). His former neighbours and townspeople of Nazareth had contemptuously dismissed Him with the words "Is not this Joseph's son?" They had wanted to kill Him by throwing Him over the brow of a hill. The opposition steadily grew as the Saviour began to preach, teach, and heal. Soon He would experience fierce hatred from the leaders of the nation. This antagonism came chiefly from the three groups, which comprised the ruling class, viz., the scribes, the Pharisees and the Sadducees. They all alike despised Jesus of Nazareth.

The scribes were known for their rigid adherence to the minutiae of the Law. They went beyond what Moses had commanded and turned the Law into tedium. The Pharisees, who were a strict religious sect within Judaism, were characterised by hypocrisy. The Sadducees, on the other hand, were the liberals of their day, refusing to believe in spirit or resurrection. However, they all had this much in common - they increasingly hated the Nazarene. Together they had to face the most important question - Who was Jesus of Nazareth? Was He the Messiah of Israel, the Christ of God? Was He the One for whom the nation had been waiting? They had been expecting a liberator who would break the Roman yoke.

Their perceptions of the Messiah were highly political, but Jesus of Nazareth was not like that. In fact, he was calling men to repentance and faith and was eating and drinking with such undesirables as tax collectors and sinners. He spoke of heaven and hell, sin and salvation. More seriously, He said that God was His Father and that He had come down from heaven. He made various astounding claims about Himself, saying that He was greater than Jonah (Mat 12:41); greater than Solomon (Mat 12:42); and greater than the temple (Mat 12:6). He claimed to be the Way, the Truth and the Life (John 14:6); the Light of the World (John 8:12); the Bread of Life (John 6:35); the Water of Life (John 4:14); the Good Shepherd (John 10:11); the Door of Salvation (John 10:9); the Resurrection and the Life (John 11:25); and the True Vine (John 15:1). Further, He claimed to be equal with the Father (John 5:17 ff.); to have authority to forgive sins

(Mk 2:10); to be the Giver of eternal life (John 10:27); to have existed before His birth (John 17:5); to have come down from heaven (John 6:38); and that His death would be atoning (Mk 10:45). Perhaps most astounding of all, the Lord Jesus claimed to be above all (John 3:31), and to be the Judge of all mankind (Mat 25:31-46). This was not what they wanted to hear.

The Rulers' rejection of Christ

How then did the rulers respond to such claims? As leaders of the nation, they would have to make a formal assessment of this Man. He could not be ignored. Sadly, the rulers totally rejected the Lord Jesus and His words. So much so, that they variously described the Saviour as a deceiver (John 7:12); possessed of a demon (John7:20); a false witness (John 8:13); a Samaritan (John 8:48); a man not of God (John 9:16); a Sabbath breaker (John 9:16); a sinner (John 9:24); a madman (John 10:20); a blasphemer (John 10:33); deserving of death (John 11:53); a criminal (John 18:30); working by the power of Beelzebub (Mat 12:24); deserving of crucifixion (Mat 27:23); a sham Saviour (Luke 23:35); a false Christ (Luke 23:35); and a false King (Luke 23:37).

Soon the rulers were plotting His death. However, they had a problem in that they needed a pretext to put the Lord to death. There was absolutely nothing with which they could charge Him. The rulers had set all kinds of traps for Him so that they could accuse Him. They had asked Him questions about the Law of Moses, and about paying taxes to Caesar, hoping that He would say something which could be construed as wrong or seditious. Luke tells us that "they watched him, and sent forth spies, which would feign themselves just men, that they might take hold of his words, that so they might deliver him unto the power and authority of the governor" (Luke 20:20). Much to the annoyance of the Pharisees and the chief priests, on one occasion the very officers sent to arrest Him had to confess "Never man spake like this man" (John 7:46).

The leaders were under no misapprehension that the Lord Jesus was a good man. However, if they could manage to have

Him put to death as a criminal or blasphemer, then they could be confident, in their perverse way of thinking, that He never was the Messiah. A good man was expendable if it meant they could hold on to their own power. John records for us the thinking behind their plotting:

"Then gathered the chief priests and the Pharisees a council, and said, What do we? for this man doeth many miracles. If we let him thus alone, all men will believe on him: and the Romans shall come and take away both our place and nation. And one of them named Caiaphas, being the high priest that same year, said unto them, Ye know nothing at all, nor consider that it is expedient for us, that one man should die for the people, and that the whole nation perish not. And this spake he not of himself: but being high priest that year, he prophesied that Jesus should die for that nation; and not for that nation only, but that also he should gather together the children of God that were scattered abroad. Then from that day forth they took counsel together for to put him to death" (John 11:47-53).

On arresting the Lord Jesus in the Garden of Gethsemane, the Jews brought Him firstly to the house of Annas, and then to the house of the high priest Caiaphas. The scribes and elders had assembled for the mock trial, and false witnesses had been lined up to accuse Him. The blessed Lord stood in silent dignity as men wickedly lied about Him. He answered nothing until Caiaphas said, "I adjure thee by the living God, that thou tell us whether thou be the Christ, the Son of God" (Mat 26:63). By doing so, the high priest had invoked the oath of Leviticus 5:1 "If any one sins in that he hears a public adjuration to testify, and though he is a witness, whether he has seen or come to know the matter, yet does not speak, he shall bear his iniquity" (*ESV*). According to this Mosaic requirement, a witness could not remain silent when he heard a public adjuration to testify - to do so would be a sin. The Lord Jesus of course always observed the law of Moses and at that point duly answered the high priest's question. Mark records the Lord's answer "I am: and ye shall see the Son of man sitting on the right hand of power, and coming in the clouds of heaven" (Mk 14:62). At this point, the court became incensed, the high priest tore his robes, and the people began to mock and wickedly abuse Him.

There was a violent and shocking reaction to the Lord's claim to Deity and to His use of the title 'Son of man'. Each person in that court would instantly have recognised the allusion to Daniel's words "I saw in the night visions, and, behold, one like the Son of man came with the clouds of heaven, and came to the Ancient of days, and they brought him near before him" (Dan 7:13). The 'Son of man' is the Lord's great Messianic title. By answering the question in this way, the Lord Jesus was publicly and unmistakably claiming to be the 'Son of man' of Daniel's vision. The Jews accused Him of blasphemy, spat in His face, and condemned Him to death.

There were, in total, six separate trials of the Lord Jesus, three of them Jewish and three of them Gentile. The three Jewish trials took place firstly in the house of Annas, then in the house of Caiaphas, and thirdly, early in the morning before the Sanhedrin. The Gentile trials took place before Pilate the Governor, then before King Herod, and finally back before Pilate. Sadly the Governor, who acknowledged three times that he could find no fault with "Jesus who is called Christ", yielded to the pressures put on him by the Jews, and passed the death sentence. This was nothing less than judicial murder. Pilate had acceded to the worst miscarriage of justice in the whole of human history, or indeed that ever could be.

After the scourging and abuse at the hands of the Roman soldiers, they led Jesus of Nazareth outside the walls of Jerusalem to the place called Calvary, where they crucified Him. As they looked at the Lord Jesus Christ nailed to the cross between two criminals, it must have seemed to the rulers that they had now settled the question once and for all - that Jesus of Nazareth was not, and never could have been, the Messiah. In a few hours He would be dead and that would be the end of Him. Indeed their wicked glee knew no bounds as they continued to taunt Him even when He was on the cross. The rulers mocked Him with the words "He saved others; let him save himself, if he be Christ, the chosen of God" (Lu 23:35).

The Roman soldiers also joined in the derision by saying "If thou be the king of the Jews, save thyself" (Lu 23:36-37). How did the Lord Jesus react to the actions of those who had carried out this murderous deed? His words of unparalleled grace sounded out majestically from the cross and have echoed down the centuries ever since, "Father, forgive them; for they know not what they do" (Luke 23:34).

Before we leave that dreadful scene of Golgotha, we must take careful note of the triumphant cry of the Lord Jesus before He dismissed His spirit, "It is finished" (John 19:30). Exactly what was *finished*? The word means: ended, completed, executed, concluded, exhausted, discharged, and performed. First, all the scriptures concerning His death were fulfilled. Second, the Lord Jesus had glorified His Father on the earth and had finished the work that He had given Him to do. Third, all the work necessary for *our salvation* was accomplished. The great work of putting away sin had been finished forever by His one, single, never-to-be-repeated sacrifice. Redemption had now been assured by the shedding of the blood of Christ. The debt was discharged, the ransom had been fully paid. Because of the finished work of Christ, God could now deal with the whole world in grace. The cry *"finished"* ushered in the day of salvation and the age of grace. Erich Sauer has expressed the truth in these striking words: "the shameful deed at the cross became by redemption the turning point of human history and of the whole drama of universal super-history".

Events after the Cross

On the day following the crucifixion, when the body of the Lord Jesus lay in Joseph's new tomb, the chief priests and the Pharisees asked Pilate that the tomb might be secured and sealed, on the pretext that His disciples might steal the body and dupe the people that He had risen from the dead. On obtaining Pilate's permission, they "made the sepulchre sure, sealing the stone, and setting a watch" (Mat 27:66).

The chief priests, however, were soon to receive alarming news. Some of the guards who had been assigned to the tomb came to the priests and told them of strange events which they had witnessed. There had been an earthquake, and some kind of supernatural being had appeared and rolled back the stone from the door of the tomb. The guards had trembled in fear as this Being, whom Matthew records as being the angel of the Lord, proceeded to sit on the stone. His appearance was like lightning and his clothing was white as snow. The guards were traumatised beyond words and became "as dead men" (Mat 28:4). While the guards were in deep shock, the angel said to the women "Fear not ye: for I know that ye seek Jesus, which was crucified. He is not here: for he is risen, as he said. Come, see the place where the Lord lay. And go quickly, and tell his disciples that he is risen from the dead; and, behold, he goeth before you into Galilee; there shall ye see him: lo, I have told you" (Mat 28:5-7).

When the women had left the tomb, and the angel of the Lord had departed, we can imagine the fear and dismay of the guards. On mustering up a little courage, they doubtless checked the tomb for themselves. Their worst fears would have been confirmed. The body had gone, and they were in deep trouble. It was then that some of the guards had made their way to Jerusalem to report the happenings to the chief priests. There was a full meeting of the Sanhedrin at which they decided what their policy toward the idea of a risen Christ ought to be. They paid the soldiers a large sum of money to lie about the events, and we read the sad words "So they took the money, and did as they were taught: and this saying is commonly reported among the Jews until this day" (Mat 28:15).

It would seem the chief priests and rulers did not consider for a single moment the possibility that the Lord Jesus had *really* risen from the dead. They did not objectively investigate the guards' evidence, nor did they consider the implications of the eyewitness accounts. Their minds were made up and their hearts were hardened. They would continue in their total and absolute rejection of Jesus of Nazareth, even if it meant bribing men to lie.

Let us leave the Jews for a moment and consider the impact

of these events on the Lord's disciples. They too were bewildered by His death. It seemed to convey the very thing that the rulers had wanted to prove - that Jesus of Nazareth could not have been the Messiah. This is evident from the conversation between the two disciples who were walking to Emmaus on that resurrection Sunday. They were talking together about all the things that had happened, when in the beautiful words of Luke, "Jesus himself drew near, and went with them" (Luke 24:15). The disciples did not know that it was the Lord. On His invitation, they proceeded to explain their perplexity to Him. They described how Jesus of Nazareth had been a prophet mighty in deed and word before God and all the people, and how the chief priests and rulers had Him condemned and crucified. Their hopes that He had been the Messiah and Redeemer of their nation were now in ruins. But soon the Lord Jesus had taken over the conversation and was expounding "unto them in all the scriptures the things concerning himself" (Luke 24:27). The risen Saviour, still unrecognised by the disciples, then explained something that neither the rulers nor the disciples had properly understood - that it was *necessary* for "Christ to have suffered these things, and to enter into his glory" (Luke 24:26).

The discourse ended when the Lord Jesus made Himself known to them in the breaking of bread, at which point He vanished out of their sight. That same day, when the two disciples had returned to Jerusalem and had joined the eleven, we read, "Jesus himself stood in the midst of them". The Lord reassured the frightened disciples by showing them His hands and His feet to demonstrate that He was neither spirit nor ghost. After eating before them, He continued to speak on the same theme that He had commenced in Emmaus - the reason for His suffering and death. The Lord's explanation of events is of the greatest importance: "These are the words which I spake unto you, while I was yet with you, that all things must be fulfilled, which were written in the law of Moses, and in the prophets, and in the psalms, concerning me....Thus it is written, and thus *it behoved Christ to suffer*, and to rise from the dead the third day: and that repentance and remission of sins should be preached in his name among all nations, beginning at Jerusalem. And ye are witnesses of these things" (Luke 24:44-48). At last, the crucifixion of Jesus of Nazareth was beginning to make sense to the disciples.

The resurrection appearances of the Lord Jesus continued for forty days. It is interesting to note that He did not appear to unbelievers, but to believers only. The last time that this world had sight of Christ was when He was nailed to the cross. The next time that this world will see Christ will be on His second coming as foretold by the Lord Himself "And then shall appear the sign of the Son of man in heaven: and then shall all the tribes of the earth mourn, and they shall see the Son of man coming in the clouds of heaven with power and great glory" (Mat 24:30).

The final appearance of those forty days took place at Bethany, close to Jerusalem. The disciples were still concerned with the question of the restoration of the kingdom to Israel and asked the Lord if it would take place at that time. The Lord Jesus gently told them that it was not for them to know the times or the seasons that the Father had fixed by His own authority. True, the kingdom would one day be restored to Israel, but that lay out in the future. The disciples now had a different mission in the world. They were to be witnesses to Christ at Jerusalem, Judea, Samaria, and the uttermost parts of the earth. They were to wait at Jerusalem until they would be baptised with the Holy Spirit "not many days hence" (Acts 1:5), thus receiving the power to witness. Having said these things, and while the disciples were watching, the Lord Jesus ascended until a cloud received Him out of their sight. He had come from God and was going to God. He had finished the work on earth that His Father had given Him to do. Our blessed Lord Jesus Christ "was received up into heaven, and sat on the right hand of God" (Mk 16:19).

The Day of Pentecost

The promise of the Father came on the Day of Pentecost,

exactly fifty days after the Feast of Firstfruits when the Lord Jesus had risen from the dead and had become the Firstfruits of them that slept. On the Day of Pentecost the Holy Spirit came down from heaven to indwell believers, and to convince the world of sin, righteousness and judgement (John 16:8). The Jews in Jerusalem reacted with amazement when they heard the disciples speaking in many different languages. Some asked what it all meant, while others mocked and attributed the phenomenon to new wine! Peter gave the explanation that this outpouring of the Holy Spirit had been foretold by the prophet Joel. Peter went on to charge the nation with the crucifixion of Christ:

"Ye men of Israel, hear these words; Jesus of Nazareth, a man approved of God among you by miracles and signs, which God did by him in the midst of you, as ye yourselves also know: Him, being delivered by the determinate counsel and foreknowledge of God, ye have taken, and by wicked hands have crucified and slain: whom God hath raised up, having loosed the pains of death: because it was not possible that he should be holden of it...Therefore let all the house of Israel know assuredly, that God hath made that same Jesus, whom ye have crucified, both Lord and Christ" (Acts 2:22-24,36).

Alarmed at the enormity of the accusation, the people asked Peter and the others what they ought to do. The news was good in that God was giving them an opportunity to repent. Peter replied, "Repent, and be baptised everyone of you in the name of Jesus Christ for the remission of sins, and ye shall receive the gift of the Holy Ghost" (Acts 2:37-38). We are informed that on that day about three thousand people gladly received his Word and were baptised. These new converts continued steadfastly in the apostles' doctrine and fellowship, and in breaking of bread and prayers. In fact, people were being saved every day, and the Lord added such to the church (Acts 2:47).

The Sanhedrin's first official rejection of Christ

The authorities would quickly need to formulate an official

policy toward this new movement, which would soon become known as "the way". Yet another event was about to happen which would rock the authorities. Peter and John, on going into the temple to pray, had healed a lame man in the name of Jesus Christ of Nazareth. The man, who had been lame from birth, followed Peter and John into the temple "walking, and leaping, and praising God" (Acts 3:8). An inquisitive crowd soon gathered in Solomon's Porch to investigate the healed man's newfound agility. Peter, taking good advantage of the situation, addressed the people of Jerusalem and revealed the truth about the miracle and its implications. Denying that the man's healing had anything to do with their power or holiness, Peter continued with the solemn charge: "The God of Abraham, and of Isaac, and of Jacob, the God of our fathers, hath glorified his Son Jesus; whom ye delivered up, and denied him in the presence of Pilate, when he was determined to let him go. But ye denied the Holy One and the Just, and desired a murderer to be granted unto you; and killed the Prince of life, whom God hath raised from the dead; whereof we are witnesses" (Acts 3:13-15).

Peter went on to explain that they had acquiesced in His death through ignorance: "And now, brethren, I wot that through ignorance ye did it, as did also your rulers." How horribly wrong they had been in joining with their rulers in demanding the crucifixion of Christ. They too had swallowed the lie that if Jesus of Nazareth was put to death, then He could not have been the Messiah. However, Peter had news for them. By putting Him to death, they had actually fulfilled prophecy:

"But those things, which God before had shewed by the mouth of all his prophets, that *Christ should suffer*, he hath so fulfilled" (Acts 3:18).

This truth, which was expounded by the Lord Jesus to the disciples on the road to Emmaus, would now become the central emphasis of the gospel message to the Jews. It would later be taken up by Paul when preaching in the Jewish synagogues. What was God's attitude to people who had crucified His Son? We can now observe the answer to the Lord's prayer on the cross when He said "Father, forgive them; for they know not what they do" (Luke 23:34). Peter proclaimed the gracious offer "Repent ye therefore, and be converted, that your sins may be blotted out..." In his address to the people, Peter claimed that Jesus Christ was the Prophet of whom Moses and the prophets had spoken. It magnifies the grace of God to think that the very people in whose city Christ was crucified, were the first to receive the offer of repentance and forgiveness: "Unto you first God, having raised up his Son Jesus, sent him to bless you, in turning away every one of you from his iniquities" (Acts 3:26).

Peter's temple sermon was soon to be interrupted by the priests, the captain of the temple, and the Sadducees. When they heard the apostles proclaiming the resurrection from the dead they had them arrested and put in prison. Up to this point, Peter had been addressing the common people in the temple. Now he would bear witness before the rulers of the nation.

The court hearing was arranged for the following day. The company which assembled that next morning consisted of rulers, elders, scribes, Annas the high priest, Caiaphas, John, Alexander, and "as many as were of the kindred of the high priest" (Acts 4:5-6). Peter and John were brought into the court and were ordered to give an explanation as to the healing of the lame man. "By what power, or by what name, have ye done this?" demanded the court.

Peter answered the question with the gravest of accusations against the rulers, and with an uncompromising statement of truth concerning the One whom they had crucified:

"Ye rulers of the people, and elders of Israel, if we this day be examined of the good deed done to the impotent man, by what means he is made whole; be it known unto you all, and to all the people of Israel, that by the name of Jesus Christ of Nazareth, whom ye crucified, whom God raised from the dead, even by him doth this man stand here before you whole. This is the stone which was set at naught of you builders, which is become the head of the corner. Neither is there salvation in any other: for there is none other name under heaven given among men, whereby we must be saved" (Acts 4:8-12).

The rulers marvelled at the boldness of Peter and John, not least because they were obviously uneducated men. Interestingly, what they *did* recognise was that they "had been with Jesus".

There was also another factor that completely embarrassed and irritated the authorities. They could not deny anything Peter had said, because the living proof was standing in their midst - the man who had been healed. Peter, John, and the healed man were taken out of the room while the court conferred. This was a defining moment in the life of the nation, when they would have to decide on an official policy towards Jesus of Nazareth. Should they acknowledge that they had crucified their King and thus lead the nation in repentance toward God, or should they insist that Jesus of Nazareth was a deceiver and that they had been right to crucify Him?

Luke allows us to eavesdrop on the deliberations that ensued. Perplexed with their dilemma, they asked, "What shall we do to these men? for that indeed a notable miracle has been done by them is manifest to all them that dwell in Jerusalem; and we cannot deny it." What an extraordinary admission! So what should be done? Sadly and tragically, they decided to persist in their official rejection of Christ. They came to an agreement as to how they would deal with the apostles: "But that it spread no further among the people, let us straitly threaten them, that they speak henceforth to no man in this name" (Acts 4:17). Thus, the rulers missed their opportunity for national repentance, and instead endorsed their earlier rejection of Christ. In so doing, they led the nation headlong into a time of desolation, unbelief, and blindness, which continues to this present day (see Romans 11:25).

Having made their infernal choice, the rulers brought the apostles back into the court and ordered them "not to speak at all nor teach in the name of Jesus". Peter and John made their famous reply: "Whether it be right in the sight of God to hearken unto you more than unto God, judge ye. For we cannot but speak the things which we have seen and heard" (Acts 4:18-20). After further threats, the Jews finally let the apostles go, not being able to find any reasonable pretext to punish them. They were scared of the possible reaction of the people who were highly impressed by what had been done among them. In fact, five thousand men had believed, adding to the three thousand who had believed on the Day of Pentecost. The man on whom the miracle was done had now become a loud and powerful voice to the city of Jerusalem.

The Sanhedrin's second official rejection of Christ

It would not be long before the Jewish Sanhedrin would meet formally to deliberate for a second time on the subject of Jesus of Nazareth and His followers. It appears to have been the custom for the apostles in those early days to gather daily in Solomon's porch, a precinct of the temple. Not only were signs and wonders being done by the apostles among the people of Jerusalem, but also those from the surrounding cities were taking their sick friends to Jerusalem for blessing. We are told that "they were healed every one" (Acts 5:16). Increasing numbers of the common people were turning to the Lord, and Luke informs us that "believers were the more added to the Lord, multitudes both of men and women" (Acts 5:14).

Incensed with anger, the high priest and the Sadducees had the apostles arrested and put in the common prison. The next morning the Sanhedrin gathered together to deal with the apostles. Luke informs us that the high priest, and those with him, called the council together and "all the senate of the children of Israel" (Acts 5:21). On the assembling of this illustrious company, the prisoners were sent for. Imagine the shock and consternation of the officers when the prison doors were opened and the cell was found to be empty! On returning to the high priest, they reported that they had found the prison properly secured with the guards still on duty, but upon opening the doors, they had found "no man within". They could offer no rational explanation for this impossible and unnatural event. While the chief priests and the temple captain were wondering to what this might lead, news came to them that the apostles were standing in the temple teaching the people.

What had happened? We read that the angel of the Lord had opened the prison doors at night and had brought the apostles out, charging them to go to the temple and speak to the people "all the words of this life". It was surely no accident that such a seemingly impossible event took place while the Sadducees were in power. It was the Sadducees who did not believe in the resurrection of the body. For them the idea of Jesus of Nazareth vacating a sealed tomb was an impossible and ridiculous idea. Miracles like that, according to them, simply did not happen in real life. Now they had been completely baffled and silenced. How could they now mock the idea of the resurrection of Christ out of a sealed tomb, when a similar miracle had undeniably occurred right in front of them and under their jurisdiction? The Sadducees were now faced with a perplexing question about the person of Christ. Could it be that they had been wrong, and that in fact Christ *had* risen from the dead and had come out of that tomb, even though it had been sealed and guarded, just as the prison doors had been locked and guarded? Their rationalistic rejection of resurrection had been turned to ridicule.

The temple captain and his officers arrested the apostles in the temple, though without violence for fear of the people, and brought them before the council. The high priest began the proceedings by asking: "Did not we straitly command you that ye should not teach in this name? And, behold, ye have filled Jerusalem with your doctrine, and intend to bring this man's blood upon us" (Acts 5:28). Peter's answer is full of significance, not only for Jews in general, but perhaps for Sadducees in particular. Peter replied, "We ought to obey God rather than men. The God of our fathers *raised up Jesus*, whom ye slew and hanged on a tree. Him hath God exalted with his right hand to be a Prince and a Saviour, for to give repentance to Israel, and forgiveness of sins. And we are witnesses of these things; and so is also the Holy Ghost, whom God hath given to them that obey him" (Acts 5:29-32).

This is a truly remarkable presentation of gospel truth in a few words. We have the fact of Christ's death on the tree, His resurrection and exaltation as Saviour, and the offer of repentance to Israel and forgiveness of sins. It is important to note that here the repentance is being offered to Israel. This echoes the words of the Lord Jesus to the disciples that "repentance and remission of sins should be preached in his name among all nations, beginning at Jerusalem" (Luke 24:47). The Sanhedrin, as rulers of Israel, would have to make an official response to this. There were only two choices open to them. Their first option was to acknowledge that they had made a horrendous mistake in rejecting their King, and that He had, in spite of all that the Sadducees had taught, been raised from the dead. Their second option was to close their eyes to the evidence and to persist in their unbelief and rejection of Christ.

The Sanhedrin, instead of calling the nation to repentance, led the people yet further astray. We read that they were cut to the heart and "took council to slay them." It was Gamaliel, a respected doctor and Pharisee, who persuaded the council to spare the apostles' lives. The Sanhedrin relented and instead made do with physically punishing the apostles and releasing them, charging them not to speak in the name of Jesus. And so, for the second time the rulers of Israel had made a formal rejection of Christ.

The Sanhedrin's third official rejection of Christ

There was to be one more and final time when the rulers of Israel would have to make an official decision about Christ and His claims. On this third occasion, it was not the apostles who were on trial, but a disciple called Stephen. The background is given by Luke: "And the word of God increased; and the number of disciples multiplied in Jerusalem greatly; and a great number of the priests were obedient to the faith. And Stephen, full of faith and power, did great wonders and miracles among the people" (Acts 6:7-8). The opposition to Stephen came mainly from members of a particular synagogue in Jerusalem that catered for Jews from Cyrene, Alexandria, Cilicia, and Asia. Unable to withstand the wisdom of Stephen, they had hired false witnesses to lie against him. They then "stirred up the people, and the elders, and the scribes, and came upon him, and brought him to the council" (Acts 6:12). The false witnesses told their lies while the Sanhedrin watched and listened for Stephen's response.

Stephen recited the course and spirit of the nation's history from the moment that its founding father Abraham had seen the God of glory, to the time of the death of Christ. As Stephen spoke, a recurring theme began to emerge in this history lesson. Each time God had sent deliverers, the nation had rejected them. Notwithstanding, on each occasion God had overruled in grace. The story of Joseph was a case in point. Joseph's brothers had wronged him grievously by selling him into slavery, yet God overruled so that Joseph one day became the means of their deliverance. Similarly Moses, who had been misunderstood and rejected by his countrymen when he had delivered the Israelite from the Egyptian, had been sent by God to be a deliverer of the nation. Further, the nation's perception of Deity had become so narrow and distorted that they had thought the God of heaven was confined to their temple in Jerusalem. But even Solomon had realised that God was infinitely greater than His temple in Jerusalem.

However, the main point of the history lesson was yet to come. The many crimes that their fathers had committed were now being repeated and grossly outdone by Stephen's generation. Just as their fathers had refused Joseph and Moses, so this generation had refused the very Christ of God. Stephen summed up with the most solemn of accusations: "Ye stiffnecked and uncircumcised in heart and ears, ye do always resist the Holy Ghost: as your fathers did, so do ye. Which of the prophets have not your fathers persecuted? and they have slain them which shewed before of the coming of the Just One; of whom ye have been now the betrayers and murderers: who have received the law by the disposition of angels, and have not kept it" (Acts 7:51-53).

On this occasion the Sanhedrin did not hold any secret conference. When Stephen claimed to see the heavens opened and the Son of man standing on the right hand of God, they immediately shouted him down, dragged him out of the city and stoned him to death. By murdering Stephen they had sent their final answer back to heaven. For the third time the Sanhedrin had formally endorsed the crucifixion of Christ. They would not repent, and they would have none of Christ. As a nation they had, as it were, signed, sealed and stamped their diabolical decision.

But although God would henceforth suspend His dealings with Israel as His covenant people, He would still save individual Jews on the same ground as individual Gentiles. Interestingly, there was a Pharisee standing there that day who fully endorsed the murder of Stephen, but who was soon to become God's great pattern convert, namely Saul of Tarsus. Paul would later reflect on those days in his letter to Timothy: "This is a faithful saying, and worthy of all acceptation, that Christ Jesus came into the world to save sinners; of whom I am chief. Howbeit for this cause I obtained mercy, that in me first Jesus Christ might shew forth all longsuffering, for a pattern to them which should hereafter believe on him to life everlasting" (1 Tim 1:15-16).

The Sequel

It should be noted that the nation could no longer plead ignorance for the murder of their Messiah. They had reasoned, in their perverse way of thinking, that if Jesus of Nazareth had died on a criminal's cross, He could not have been the Christ. But we have already noted that Peter, whilst attributing ignorance to both the common people and the rulers, called them to urgent repentance. The enormity of the crime was now fully known, and they were entirely without excuse.

When Paul was in the synagogue at Antioch of Pisidia, he likewise touched on the issue of ignorance: "Men and brethren, children of the stock of Abraham, and whosoever among you feareth God, to you is the word of this salvation sent. For they that dwell at Jerusalem, and their rulers, *because they knew him not*, nor yet the voices of the prophets which are read every Sabbath day, they have fulfilled them in condemning him.....Be it known unto you therefore, men and brethren, that through this man is preached unto you the forgiveness of sins: and by him all that believe are justified from all things, from which ye could not be justified by the law of Moses" (Acts 13:26-27, 38-39).

After the martyrdom of Stephen, a new wave of persecution began in Jerusalem. The believers, with the exception of the apostles, were scattered abroad. This would result in Samaritans, and eventually Gentiles, hearing the gospel. But God was not yet finished with the Jew. Although the offer of the kingdom had been earlier withdrawn from the nation, nevertheless it was the privilege of the Jews to hear the gospel first. When Paul went on his missionary journeys, it was always his custom to go to the Jews before going to the Gentiles. Writing to the Christians at Rome, Paul explained his missionary strategy: "For I am not ashamed of the gospel of Christ: for it is the power of God unto salvation to every one that believeth; *to the Jew first* and also to the Greek" (Rom 1:16). But sadly, the vast majority of the Jews in the cities and towns from Syria to Italy endorsed the decision made by the rulers in Jerusalem. Even so, there was a minority of Jews who did believe, a company that Paul referred to as 'the remnant' (Rom 11:5). But as for the nation of Israel, its rulers and people, the time of visitation had come and gone. Their day of opportunity as a nation was over, and the kingdom was no longer on offer. Of course individual Jews could still be saved on the same ground as individual Gentiles, but Israel as a covenant nation was set aside. The last recorded words of Paul in the Acts of the Apostles are addressed to the chief Jews at Rome: "Be it known therefore unto you, that the salvation of God is sent unto the Gentiles, and that they will hear it" (Acts 28:28).

We have already observed that the Lord Jesus had three Jewish trials and three Gentile trials. Further, Pilate protested the innocence of Christ three times to the people before he reluctantly assented to His death. And now, after the death and resurrection of Christ, God gave the Sanhedrin three definite opportunities to re-examine their role in Christ's death, to admit their grievous error and to repent. The answer from the rulers, who could no longer plead ignorance, was that they would never have Jesus of Nazareth to rule over them. After much longsuffering, God took them at their word.

The setting aside of Israel as a nation raises many important questions and issues. Has God cast off Israel forever? Has the church replaced Israel? How does Israel now relate to the covenants and promises? How do Jews now stand in relation to the gospel? In other words, what must a Jew do to be saved? The answer is clear and unambiguous. He can only be saved in exactly the same way as a Gentile can be saved, and that is by repentance toward God and faith in our Lord Jesus Christ. The Jew, like the Gentile, must acknowledge his ruin and helplessness as a guilty sinner, and rest in Christ for His forgiveness and salvation. But that is the difficult part for the Jew, to acknowledge that the despised Jesus of Nazareth, Christ crucified, is the only Saviour of sinners. It must have been a great shock to Saul of Tarsus on the Damascus road when he received the answer to his question "Who art thou Lord?" Saul heard the voice say, "I am Jesus of Nazareth, whom thou persecutest" (Acts 22:8). At that moment Saul must have realised that he had been horrendously wrong in his estimation of Christ. Happily, he was not disobedient to the heavenly vision, but in a state of trembling and astonishment, bowed his heart in repentance and faith saying: "Lord, what wilt thou have me to do?" It is no different for the Jew to-day. He too must bow his heart and believe in the Lord Jesus Christ. But that is exactly what the Jew finds so hard, and yet there is no other gospel, and no other doctrine.

CHAPTER 3

The Response of the Gentile World

In the previous chapter we observed that the majority of Jewish people reacted to the gospel message with calculated rejection and hostility, even though they had enjoyed great privilege and preservation by being made the custodians of the law. They had been sheltered, or ought to have been, from the evil excesses of pagan society. Outside of the Jewish fold, the ancient world was characterised by occult, polytheism, idolatry, philosophy and sheer hedonism. We have already noted that mankind had refused to acknowledge God as Creator and had worshipped and served the creature rather than the Creator. Professing to be wise, they had become fools. God had given them up to their own choices with the result that men were living in spiritual and moral darkness. So much so, their behaviour had become unnatural and harmful. It was into such a needy, ruined, world that the gospel light would now shine in grace and mercy. The purpose of this chapter is to investigate the various reactions to the gospel that emanated from the wider Gentile world.

We have already noted that the first non-Jews to hear and believe the gospel were Samaritans. It was the command of the Lord Jesus that the great work of evangelism, after beginning with Jerusalem and Judea, should focus on Samaria before moving out to the whole world (Acts 1:8). At this point we might well ask who the Samaritans actually were and why they came into such favour in the gracious purposes of God. What was the origin of the Samaritans?

The answer to that question takes us back over 700 years

before Christ to the mighty Assyrian empire of King Shalmaneser. The ancient Assyrians practised ethnic cleansing on a massive scale. It was their policy to remove whole nations from their lands, and to replace them with other displaced peoples. After besieging Samaria, the capital city of the northern kingdom of Israel, the Assyrians exiled the ten tribes of Israel and resettled them in Syria, Assyria, and Babylonia. This mass deportation, which according to Assyrian annals was completed by King Sargon, was followed by a repopulation of Samaria by peoples from other disturbed parts of the Assyrian empire. Thus we read that the king of Assyria brought men from "Babylon, and from Cuthah, and from Ava, and from Hamath, and from Sepharvaim, and placed them in the cities of Samaria instead of the children of Israel: and they possessed Samaria, and dwelt in the cities thereof" (see 2 Kings 17:1-41).

The new inhabitants of Samaria were idolaters who worshipped various gods, some even practising child sacrifice. When they had been in Samaria for a short time the region was overrun with lions, a phenomenon which the new inhabitants attributed to their ignorance of the God of the land. They appealed to the king of Assyria for help. The king's solution was to send to them one of the original exiled priests who would be able to teach the people "the manner of the God of the land" (2 Kings 17:27). Such a priest duly came and taught the people how they could fear the LORD. We then read of a very early example of religious syncretism by which the people "feared the LORD, and served their own gods". Thus came into being the people who were called Samaritans.

Eventually there was a complete division of Jews and Samaritans, so that when we come to the time of the Lord Jesus, the Jews had no dealings whatever with Samaritans (John 4:9). The Samaritan woman was therefore surprised when the Lord Jesus addressed her at Jacob's well. It is truly remarkable that the Saviour should speak to such a person about everlasting life and true worship. When confronted with the issue of her sin she attempted to evade the question by appealing to the different places of worship that were then in existence for

Samaritans and Jews. The Lord's response to that statement is most illuminating. Did He tell her that it did not really matter how, or where, people worship, so long as they were sincere? Did He say that there were common truths in both Judaism and Samaritanism, and that they were both equally valid? No, He said none of these things. What in fact He did say to the woman demolishes today's ideas of religious pluralism and relativism. The Lord Jesus said to her *"Ye worship ye know not what: we know what we worship: for salvation is of the Jews."*

The religious beliefs of Samaritanism were hopelessly confused and could do nothing to meet the need of guilty sinners. There was no salvation in Samaritanism, and the Lord Jesus said so. Further, the Lord stated unambiguously and definitively that salvation was of the Jews. In other words, the original Mosaic Judaism of the Bible was most definitely from God and provided a means of approach to God. Salvation in Old Testament times was based on the principle of faith in the God of Israel. Men could repent and call upon God, but it was always to the God of Israel. It was King Solomon's prayer on completing the temple that "all the people of the earth may know thy name to fear thee, as do thy people Israel" (1 Kings 8:41-43). God had made Himself known to the world through Israel by means of the scriptures, the temple, the law and the offerings. The repentant Gentile must come to the God of Israel. There was no other God and there was no other Saviour. Isaiah records the words of God "...and there is no God else beside me; a just God and a Saviour; there is none beside me. Look unto me, and be ye saved, all the ends of the earth: for I am God, and there is none else" (Isaiah 45:21-22).

It is therefore very interesting to note that when Samaritans believed the gospel, they did not receive the Holy Spirit until Peter and John came from Jerusalem and laid their hands on them. It was at the hands of *Jewish* apostles that they received the Spirit. This demonstrated clearly that Samaritanism had never been of God, but that salvation was truly of the Jews. The Samaritans acknowledged this when they submitted to the authoritative ministry of the apostles from Jerusalem. We can surely see the wisdom of God in this. It meant that Samaritan Christians could never claim any validity or authority purporting to come from their old Samaritan religion. That had to be abandoned as false and irrelevant. It was not that the Samaritans had now to become Jews. Rather, it was an acknowledgement by Samaritan believers that salvation had indeed been of the Jews. Thus there could never be Samaritan churches claiming independence in matters of doctrine or practice. They accepted the apostolic doctrine as divinely inspired and definitive. There could be 'no other doctrine'.

The Occult in Samaria

The occult was a way of life to the people of the ancient world. What happened after the laying on of hands by Peter and John shows us that the people of Samaria were no exception. Luke records that there was "a certain man named Simon, which beforetime in the same city used sorcery, and bewitched the people of Samaria, giving out that himself was some great one: to whom they all gave heed, from the least to the greatest, saying, This man is the great power of God. And to him they had regard, because that of long time he had bewitched them with their sorceries" (Acts 8:9-11).

This piece of information tells us much about the influence of the spirit world in the lives of ordinary people. The whole population was affected, from the least to the greatest. Simon had professed to believe and was baptised, yet his heart was not right before God. He had simply gone through the motions, but there was no reality. He offered the apostles money so that he too could lay hands on people that they might receive the Holy Spirit. But salvation is not something that you can buy, nor is any aspect of Christian ministry. These things are the gift of God and cannot be purchased with money. Peter could discern that Simon's heart was still in the "gall of bitterness, and in the bond of iniquity" (Acts 8:23). The Samaritan mindset would have allowed a mixture of sorcery and Christianity. After all, their ancestors had feared the LORD and worshipped their own gods. They might even have claimed that there was richness in diversity! But Peter would not tolerate such a compromise. He advised Simon to repent of his wickedness and pray God that "if perhaps the thought of thine heart may be forgiven thee."

The attraction of the occult and the fascination with the spirit world have kept men in slavery and bondage since times immemorial. But the salvation of Samaritans was freeing them at last from such chains of superstition and darkness. Many of them were no longer deceived by Simon and his ilk. But as Simon did not want to relinquish his power and influence without a fight, he tried to buy the power that the apostles appeared to have so that he could carry on his practices within the new community. He wanted to have a foot in both camps. That of course would have been disastrous for the new Samaritan believers. There could never be compromise between light and darkness.

The Occult in Cyprus

The opposition of the spirit world to the gospel could take different forms. In the case of Simon the sorcerer, the strategy was one of compromise and stealth. But there were also times when satanic opposition took the form of open hostility. Such opposition was encountered in the early stages of the first missionary journey by Paul and Barnabas. Whereas Simon had not been openly hostile to the gospel but had tried to 'join the church', there were others who expressly opposed the gospel. Such a one was Elymas, a sorcerer who lived in Cyprus.

The Roman Proconsul of Cyprus at that time was an intelligent man by the name of Sergius Paulus. He had a desire to hear the Word of God and listened intently to Paul as he proclaimed the gospel. But Elymas the magician withstood Paul and tried to turn the Proconsul away from the faith (Acts 13:8). While Paul expounded the word of God, Elymas contradicted him and argued against such things. This was no less than a clash between the forces of light and darkness, while a man's soul hung in the balance. How was Paul to handle this kind of opposition to the gospel? Did he appeal to Elymas to sit down and share the things that they had in common? Did he concede that Elymas also had an understanding of these issues which was true for him in the subjective and relative sense and which was as equally valid as Paul's understanding of truth?

We are left in no doubt as to the nature and character of Elymas' enmity toward the gospel. Paul looked him in the eye and said "O full of all subtilty and all mischief, thou child of the devil, thou enemy of all righteousness, wilt thou not cease to pervert the right ways of the Lord?" (Acts 13:10). Blindness immediately fell on Elymas and he went about looking for someone to lead him by the hand. The triumph of the power of God over the power of Satan impressed the Proconsul, who, when he saw what had happened, "believed, being astonished at the doctrine of the Lord". Sergius Paulus had understood that there could be 'no other doctrine'.

This incident would remind us of the fact that the devil is the great enemy of souls. He has been deceiving and enslaving men and women ever since the fall of Adam. The Lord Jesus informs us that the devil is "a murderer from the beginning, and has nothing to do with the truth, because there is no truth in him. When he lies, he speaks according to his own nature, for he is a liar and the father of lies" (John 8:44). What a warning to those who would dabble in the occult in its varied forms! It results in a slavery from which only God can deliver. How good it is to be able to proclaim with total confidence that the gospel is the "power of God unto salvation to every one that believeth; to the Jew first, and also to the Greek" (Rom 1:16).

The Occult in Philippi

In Philippi we see the ugly and brutal side of the occult. As Paul and his team were going to a place of prayer they were met by a slave girl who had a "spirit of divination". The owners of this girl made substantial income from her soothsaying powers. Luke informs us that she followed Paul around for many days crying, "These men are the servants of the most high God, which shew unto us the way of salvation" (Acts 16:17). Paul, being grieved and annoyed, addressed the evil spirit "I command thee in the name of Jesus Christ to come out of her." Once again the spirit world had to bow to the greater authority of the Lord Jesus Christ. In that same hour the spirit left the girl.

One might have thought that reasonably minded people should have been glad to see the girl completely free of the dark force that had possessed and enslaved her. Sadly, such was not the case. The owners of the girl were outraged that they had lost their means of income. They actually preferred the girl to be miserably oppressed by demon powers so that she could be commercially exploited. They did not have the slightest concern for the girl's best interests. The practice of occult power is a loveless and pitiless evil. Little wonder, since it comes from the devil himself.

The slave girl's owners reacted to the gospel and its saving power in open hostility and violence. They physically manhandled Paul and Silas, dragging them into the marketplace to the rulers. The accusations that they brought against Paul and Silas played on the racial and religious prejudices of the rulers. Like many before and after them, these men were masters at spin! They spoke in deliberately vague terms, setting Roman against Jew. They accused Paul and Silas of stirring up trouble in the city, and of teaching customs unlawful for Romans. The crowd in the marketplace began to act as a violent mob. The magistrates ripped the clothes off the apostles and had them scourged with "many stripes" (Acts 16:23). The apostles were then thrown into prison and the jailer was ordered to keep them as top security prisoners. On receiving this charge, the jailer put them into the inner prison with their feet fastened securely in stocks.

It might have seemed at that moment that the powers of darkness had triumphed. It would have been understandable if Paul and Silas had indulged in a little self-pity. Yet what do we find? Rather than complaining, they were actually singing praises to God, while the other prisoners listened. And yet more, God in grace had organised an earthquake! The jailer was soon trembling on his knees asking the most important question that any person could ever ask, *"Sirs, what must I do to be saved?"*

Paul's answer brings salvation within the reach of all, irrespective of race, class, culture or age: *"Believe on the Lord Jesus Christ and thou shalt be saved".* He did not tell him to become a Jew, nor to become religious, nor even to be a more faithful follower of his own religion. To believe on the Lord Jesus Christ is to rest in His finished work on the cross, and to receive Him as Saviour and Lord. Moreover, what was true for the jailer was true for each person in the house, for Paul added "and thy house". In other words, if they believed on the Lord Jesus, they too would be saved. What was true for the jailer and his household in the first century is true for us in the twenty-first century.

Notice the change that salvation made in the life of the jailer. He did something for Paul and Silas that we could safely assume he had never done before for any other prisoners! He washed their wounds and brought them into his own house for a meal. Luke informs us that the jailer "rejoiced, believing in God with all his house" (Acts 16:34). Salvation had delivered a slave girl from demon possession, and had changed a hardened jailer into a kind and sympathetic Christian. The gospel had come right into enemy territory and had set souls free of demonic tyranny.

The Occult in Ephesus

Ephesus was a city entirely given over to the worship of pagan deities and to the occult practices that always accompany such idolatry. An incident is related which would warn us not to dabble in anything to do with the spirit world. Seven itinerant Jews, described as sons of a Jewish high priest, had attempted to cast out evil spirits by invoking the name of the Lord Jesus. On one such occasion, the evil spirit had said, "Jesus I know, and Paul I know; but who are ye?" (Acts 19:15). The man who was demon possessed assaulted the seven brothers so that they fled from the house injured and naked. It is a fact that many who begin dabbling in the occult for fun or curiosity, often become traumatised by sinister events that rapidly run out of control. To use the name of Jesus merely as a kind of magic incantation was dangerous in the extreme. This incident created great fear on all the community of Ephesus and the name of the Lord Jesus was magnified.

The interesting question arises: Can people who are involved in occult practices be saved and truly delivered from demonic powers? Happily, the answer is a resounding yes! There were many converts in Ephesus who had practised magic and black arts and who had accumulated many books on such subjects. Now that these men were saved, what should they do with their books? In what appears to have been a well-organised event, they all brought the books together at a pre-arranged time and place and proceeded to destroy them on a public bonfire "before all men". Interestingly, the value of the books was estimated at the startling amount of fifty thousand pieces of silver. This incident certainly gives us clear guidance as to what we should do with such books if we have them in our possession - *burn them*! However, Ephesus was the world centre of goddess worship and would not tolerate such things without a fight. The city was soon to bare its teeth at the gospel, as we shall consider presently.

We have observed how the gospel triumphed over the powers of darkness in Samaria, Cyprus, Philippi and Ephesus. On writing to the saints in Ephesus, Paul informed them that the believers' struggle was not against flesh and blood, but rather against "principalities, against powers, against the rulers of the darkness of this world, against spiritual wickedness in high places" (Eph 6:12). To face such a formidable foe, Paul exhorts every believer to put on the whole armour of God and so withstand the wiles of the devil. The gospel can triumph in such places of darkness, and so can the individual believer. God provides the believer with all the resources that he needs. Nevertheless, to this day the occult strongly opposes the gospel and its message.

The Gospel and Polytheism

God had made Himself known to Israel as the one and only

true God. In that sense, Judaism could be described as a monotheistic belief system, in that they believed in only one God. Outside of Judaism, it would appear that the ancient world was polytheistic - in other words, they believed in the existence of many gods and deities. For example, the gods of Egypt were without number, as were those of Assyria, Babylon, Persia, Greece and Rome. Even Israel in its former history found the lure of polytheism and its idolatry to be irresistible, and had on occasions worshipped the gods of the people around them.

As the gospel went out to the 'uttermost parts of the earth', what opposition was encountered when it was first preached among such pagan communities? How did the pagan mindset cope with the uncompromising message that spoke of one God and one Mediator between God and men? Again, we turn chiefly to the Acts of the Apostles to find the answers.

Polytheism at Lystra

If we wish to see life through the eyes of a first-century pagan, we must suspend disbelief and enter a mythological world governed by a pantheon of gods and goddesses. There were deities reigning in the sky, the sea, the earth and the underworld. It was therefore to gods and goddesses that a man would turn in such times of need as sickness, famine, war, marriage, birth, life, and death. There were gods of harvest, wine, fertility, light, sun, love, beauty, trade, arts, health, and sleep, to name but some. Thus the devotee would offer divine honours and sacrifices to the particular gods he needed at any given time. His life-view could be reduced to this core belief - *if things were going well for a man, it meant that the gods were pleased; but if things were going badly, then the gods were angry.* Not surprisingly, the chief aim of a man's religious devotions was to placate and manipulate the gods. Such a belief system was loveless, producing enslavement to superstition and fear. Such was the mindset of the people of Lystra.

We have already observed how the healing of a crippled man had been a loud and powerful voice to the people of Jerusalem.

On that occasion, Peter and John had taken advantage of the divinely given opportunity to preach the gospel to the Jewish people in the temple. Interestingly, it was also the healing of a crippled man that gave Paul and Barnabas the opportunity to present the gospel to the pagan people of Lystra.

As Paul was preaching, one notable listener was a man of Lystra who had been crippled from birth. Paul, discerning that the man had faith to be healed, said in a loud voice "Stand upright on thy feet" (Acts 14:10). To the astonishment of the people, the man leaped and walked. Whereas the man in the temple had given thanks to God, these people began to praise their pagan deities. In their blindness, they concluded that Paul and Barnabas were two gods who had come down in the likeness of men. They identified Barnabas as Zeus (Roman Jupiter), who in Greek mythology was the chief of the gods. Paul was identified as Hermes (Roman Mercury), supposedly the son of Zeus and messenger of the gods. This adulation was being articulated in the regional language of Lycaonia, and neither Paul nor Barnabas appeared to be aware of what was happening until the local priest of Zeus was about to sacrifice oxen in their honour. On realizing the intentions of the people, a horrified Paul and Barnabas tore their clothes and ran in among the people to stop the misplaced worship.

What was to be said to men who sincerely believed such things? Was their religion simply one way to God among many ways? Let us listen to Paul addressing the pagan people of Lystra:

"Sirs, why do ye these things? We also are men of like passions with you, and preach unto you that ye should turn from these vanities unto the living God, which made heaven, and earth, and the sea, and all things that are therein: who in times past suffered all nations to walk in their own ways. Nevertheless he left not himself without witness, in that he did good, and gave us rain from heaven, and fruitful seasons, filling our hearts with food and gladness" (Acts 14:15-17).

Paul began his message by challenging them to use their faculty of reason: "*Why* do ye these things?" It is right and good that men should re-think the assumptions and beliefs of a lifetime. Paul wanted them to see the foolishness of giving divine honours to mortal men. "We also are men of like passion with you," pleaded Paul. Worship or veneration of men and women is foreign to scripture. What would be the right and proper response from the people of Lystra to the miracle that they had just witnessed? Did Paul encourage the people to continue in their ethnic religion, or even to blend parts of it with Christianity? Not so, for such things were vain, empty and dead.

He firstly told the people that they "should turn from these vanities". Note the term used to describe the religious practices of the people - *vanities*. In other words, those things were empty, meaningless and futile. Secondly, to what or whom should they turn? It was to none other than "the living God". What a message! In contrast to the lifeless and powerless deities of their imagination, Paul pointed them to the *living* God who made heaven, earth, sea, and everything in them. In this, we have the essence of repentance, which is a forsaking of all that is sinful and false, and a turning unto the true and living God. On another occasion, Paul had similarly reminded the Thessalonians how they had turned "to God from idols to serve the living and true God" (1 Thess 1:9).

Paul drew attention to the power of God in creation and to His government in the affairs of the nations. In times past God had allowed the nations to walk in their own ways, but even in those dark days God had ordered certain things with a view to their bearing witness to His existence and goodness. For example, the life-sustaining cycle of rain and harvests, and the continual provision of food and gladness, all bore witness to a good and caring God. Sadly, the men of Lystra, professing to be wise had become fools. It was exactly as Paul had described mankind in the first chapter of his letter to the Romans.

The message that day was uncompromising. There was only one proper response to the healing of the crippled man. They should now forsake the vanities of their pagan past, and turn to the living and true God.

There is a sad sequel to this incident at Lystra. The Jews would have preferred that the pagans continue in their blindness, rather than come to Christ. Jews from Antioch and Iconium arrived at Lystra and persuaded the people to stone Paul, leaving him for dead. The pagans, on their part, were extremely fickle in the whole matter. One moment they were honouring Paul as a god, while the next moment they were stoning him. Such is the nature and character of this world. The gospel can have no compromise with paganism. Nor can it have any compromise with modern day neo-paganism.

Philosophy at Athens

Athens was the intellectual capital of the ancient world, a city whose name is forever linked with the flowering of philosophy. Yet it was a sad Paul who observed that the city was "wholly given to idolatry" (Acts 17:16). It is interesting to note that philosophy, in spite of its lofty claims, does not necessarily free men from idolatry. The key thought underlying Greek philosophy was that the world could be explained rationally rather than mythologically. To do so, the philosophers appealed solely to human reason and logic. Although philosophy did indeed ask important questions, human reason and ingenuity could never give the right answers. The philosophers could speculate on questions about origin and destiny, about life and death, about truth and ethics, but it would take a greater than Plato to answer these questions. Happily, Paul was able to tell them of such a Person.

Listening to Paul that day were representatives of two quite different schools of philosophical thought. Luke informs us, "certain philosophers of the Epicureans, and of the Stoics, encountered him" (Acts 17:18). So what exactly was the difference between these two philosophical outlooks?

Epicurus (341-270 BC) was an Athenian philosopher who held the atomic theory of Democritus to be the true explanation of the physical world. Epicureanism was a purely materialistic philosophy, holding that the world arose from a chance conflagration and combination of atoms. There was no such thing as spirit, and there was no after-life. A man's soul died along with his body and there was no judgement to fear. Only the gods (if indeed they existed at all) were immortal, but they had no interest in mankind. Epicurus ruled out the idea of divine intervention in the formation processes of matter and life. The Epicurean therefore believed that the only reasonable thing to pursue in life was pleasure. True pleasure, and not absolute truth, was the end at which he aimed. His ideal in life was the absence of pain, and his objective was to develop a serene detachment from the trials of life. Ultimately, there was no eternal dimension to life, and no universal truth. There were no moral absolutes, morality being useful only as far as it helped to attain the maximum pleasure. At the root of the Epicurean's materialistic philosophy was the concept of meaningless, non-purposive chance, and nothing more.

The ideas of Epicureanism are once again widely held in our own times. J.V.Luce has pointed out some similarities:

"In cosmology he (Epicurus) took the view that before our world was formed the atoms composing it were streaming rapidly downwards through the infinite expanse of empty space, moving without plan or purpose...He supposed that from time to time an individual atom would spontaneously deviate by the smallest possible amount from its straight line path...The spontaneous swerving of individual atoms caused collisions and re-bounds, and set up a tangle of criss-cross motions, as a result of which atoms became bonded and hooked together to form the larger visible masses which we call sky, air, earth, and sea. The sky was viewed as a sort of container or envelope separating off our world from infinite space, and within it further aggregations of the atoms led to the successive development of plants and animals. Some of the early animals were monstrous, ill-adapted creatures that were unable to survive and propagate their species. Epicurus developed a view not unlike the Darwinian hypothesis of the 'survival of the fittest' to account for the apparent purposiveness in organic adaptations."[2]

Whereas Epicureanism tended toward chance and randomness, Stoicism tended toward fatalism. If Epicureanism was atheistic, Stoicism was pantheistic. The Stoic School was founded in Athens at the end of the fourth century by a Cypriot named Zeno (335-263 BC). The Stoics believed in a great world-god, but it was the impersonal god of reason and nature. Rejecting the atomism of Epicurus, the Stoic viewed life as a kind of continuum, and saw the world itself as an organic, living, rational soul. There were endless cosmical cycles in which the universe would be destroyed in flames, and then re-created, and destroyed yet again, and so on forever. The human soul would survive for only one of these cosmical time periods before being absorbed into the universal soul. Life was determined by nature and destiny, so that the wisest thing a man could do was to live according to natural law and reason. By doing so, he became one with nature and the world. If misfortune befell a man, it was the result of fate and could not have been different. The Stoic accepted every eventuality in life as inevitable. In other words, whatever happens, happens necessarily; and whatever is, is right! Given these assumptions, there was nothing to be gained from remorse or regret. In practical terms, such a belief system resulted in indifference to circumstances, and tended to produce men of hard, dispassionate, steely character. The concepts of love, mercy, repentance and humility were irrelevant to this man-made system of natural law and fate.

Just as the atheistic ideas of Epicureanism have resurfaced in our own times, so have the pantheistic ideas of Stoicism. Hinduism, Buddhism, and today's New Age movement, have much in common with Stoic beliefs. Again, we quote from J.V.Luce:

"The Stoic view of the world was technically a materialistic one...But they avoided a mechanistic view of the operations of

---

[2] Luce, J.V. *An Introduction to Greek Philosophy* (Thames & Hudson, London, 1992) pp.141-142.

nature. The world, they held, is the product of an active principle to which they gave various names, including Mind and God. They conceived of God as an active force, permeating the physical world, and fashioning its more passive material elements into an ordered world of separate objects. God consisted of the finest and most active forms of matter, namely fire and air, mixed together to produce a divine 'spirit' or 'fiery breath' that nourished the world from within. God goes about his work like a skilled craftsman...But the analogy of the craftsman should not mislead us into separating the Stoic God from the material in which he works. For the Stoics, God was not above or outside the world imposing form on matter like a human designer. God was in the world and part of the world just as surely as soul was included in body. They proclaimed a pantheistic creed."[3]

The people who listened to Paul that day in Athens were a representative sample of the ancient Gentile world. Remarkably, the very same mix would be true of today's twenty-first century Gentile world. There were polytheists who believed in a multiplicity of gods; there were atheists who believed in no God; and there were pantheists who believed that everything was God. Standing on Mars' Hill, Paul had this to say to the philosophers of Athens:

"Ye men of Athens, I perceive that in all things ye are too superstitious. For as I passed by, and beheld your devotions, I found an altar with this inscription, TO THE UNKNOWN GOD.

Whom therefore ye ignorantly worship, him declare I unto you. God that made the world and all things therein, seeing he is Lord of heaven and earth, dwelleth not in temples made with hands; neither is worshipped with men's hands, as though he needed any thing, seeing he giveth to all life, and breath, and all things; and hath made of one blood all nations of men for to dwell on all the face of the earth, and hath determined the times before appointed, and the bounds of their

---

[3] Ibid p.134.

habitation; that they should seek the Lord, if haply they might feel after him, though he be not far from every one of us: for in him we live, and move, and have our being; as certain also of your own poets have said, 'For we are also his offspring'. Forasmuch then as we are the offspring of God, we ought not to think that the Godhead is like unto gold, or silver, or stone, graven by art and man's device. And the times of this ignorance God winked at; but now commandeth all men every where to repent: because he hath appointed a day, in the which he will judge the world in righteousness by that man whom he hath ordained; whereof he hath given assurance unto all men, in that he hath raised him from the dead" (Acts 17:22-31).

Some years ago, my wife and I had a holiday in Sicily where we spent a day visiting the Greek temples at Agrigento. After a walk around the ruins in the sweltering sun, we retired to the cooler sanctuary of the adjacent museum. During our tour of the museum, the Italian guide pointed to a particular exhibit and asked the group of tourists if any one could guess what it was. Our attention was drawn to a small sculpture that consisted of nothing more than a featureless pillar with a pair of carved ears. We stared intently, wondering what this miniature pillar with ears could be. After some moments of silence, the guide informed us that it was a small domestic version of the altar to the unknown God that we read about in the Bible! He went on to explain that no one knew what this God looked like, hence there was no carving of body torso or facial features. The Greeks had simply carved ears on the pillar in the hope that this unknown God would hear them.

That may, or may not, give us a clue to the possible appearance of the altar that Paul observed during his walk-around tour of Athens. At any rate, whatever it may have looked like, Paul used the altar and its inscription as a point of contact with the Athenians. The beginning of his message was that the God they worshipped in ignorance could *now be known*. What followed was a statement of truth that demolished the ideas of Epicureanism and Stoicism.

Paul proclaimed God to be the Creator of all things, and Lord of heaven and earth. Thus the Epicurean, with his materialistic universe, had missed the mark completely. The Stoic, with his impersonal god of nature, would have been shocked and jolted to hear Paul speak of a *living, infinite, personal* God. Not only had He created all things, but He was also the universal Sovereign, the Creator and Sustainer of life. He was far above the thoughts and imagination of men. Paul also informed his audience that it was God who had appointed beforehand the times and boundaries of peoples, nations, and empires. In other words, it was neither blind chance nor the laws of nature, but *God* who controlled history. Nor was His government of men despotic or arbitrary, but with the purpose in view that men might seek the Lord. Further, He is near to each one of us. Our life, our activities and our very being are in Him, in the sense that all these things are God's gifts to men. The Stoic believed in a god of nature, a force working everywhere, conscious and thinking, yet impersonal. However, one of their own poets had been closer to the mark when he wrote, "For we are also his offspring". In other words, the pantheist was wrong to say that 'everything is God'. We are not part of God, but rather we are His offspring. God is not part of the creation, and men are not part of God. There is a chiasmic difference between the Creator and His creation. Whether consciously or not, the Stoic poet had stumbled on a vital truth. An appreciation of this truth, said Paul, makes it very inappropriate to portray God in man-made idols of gold, silver or stone.

What were the implications for those men who had been living in relative ignorance of the true God? What were they now to do? Paul provided the answer by stating that God "now commandeth all men every where to repent". We should note three vital elements in this statement. First, the call to repentance is *now*. Second, the call is given in the form of an ultimatum: God now *commandeth* all men everywhere to repent. Third, the scope of this command is all-inclusive and universal: it is to *all men everywhere*. This cut across the Epicurean idea that life was based on meaningless chance. It also cut across the Stoic idea that men were powerless to alter their destiny in a fatalistic world. All men everywhere could and must repent. God commanded it!

Paul went on to tell the Athenians that God had appointed a day for world judgement. The Greek philosophers had debated much about ethics and behaviour and had concluded, in the main, that morality was relative and not absolute. For the Epicurean, the idea of ethics was simply something that would help him to avoid pain and to attain pleasure. For the Stoic, ethics meant accepting his fate and living according to the laws of nature. Paul told them that on that appointed day, God would judge the world in *righteousness*. That was what the Greeks needed to hear. There are indeed such things as moral absolutes - one is called 'righteousness.'

There is no truth as frightful and disturbing to unrighteous men as that of being personally accountable to God on an appointed day of judgement. The question could well have been put to Paul at that moment as to what his evidence was for such a weighty and unwelcome assertion. On what ground could he say such things, and what was his authority? It is at this point that Paul comes to the central truth of the gospel message, which is that salvation is in a Person. Everything he had said so far had been leading up to this gospel truth. God will judge this world by *a man whom he hath ordained*. Paul then quotes his reason for such a colossal claim: "whereof he hath given assurance unto all men, in that *he hath raised him from the dead*". We can scarcely begin to appreciate the far-reaching and eternal implications that this truth holds for the world. In a definite place, and at a certain time in the history of this world, a man who had been dead and buried was raised to life. There could be no greater sign or evidence of the voice and power of God to men. The world could never be the same again. The sin-atoning death on the cross, the burial, and the resurrection of the Lord Jesus Christ is the mighty and full provision that God has made for all men. True, Paul is not recorded as having said so on that occasion, but that does not mean that he did not preach a full gospel to the men of Athens. What Luke has recorded for us in Acts 17, is the ultimatum aspect of the gospel.

It is a command to repentance. In other words, they were to turn from all that was unrighteous and false, and turn to the One whom God had raised from the dead. The message is exactly the same today for modern men.

What did the idolaters, with their mythological worldview, think of Paul's message? What went through the minds of the Epicureans as they heard Paul speak of an after-life and world judgement? How did the Stoics respond to such concepts as righteousness and bodily resurrection? It seems to have been on the topic of resurrection that Paul's audience began to express their opinions. Some resorted to that most detestable of responses, in that they *mocked*. Others promised to hear Paul again on the subject. Happily there were some others who, with due urgency, joined Paul there and then, believing the gospel that he preached.

The polytheist's mythological idea of God was a figment of his own imagination. The Epicurean's refusal to acknowledge God had rendered him a fool. The Stoic's idea of God as the impersonal law of nature could hardly have been further from the truth. How refreshing it is to be able to proclaim the living, infinite, personal God of the Bible who has made Himself known in the Person of His Son. The very heart and character of God were revealed at Calvary's cross. Because of Calvary, God is able to forgive sinners. Those who put their faith in Christ are saved from that appointed judgement day of the great white throne. Why? - Because for the believer the judgement is already passed, having been completed at the cross on the sinner's behalf. In other words, the Lord Jesus took the sinner's place and bore his judgement. This gospel truth was expressed by the Saviour, when He said: "Verily, verily, I say unto you, He that heareth my word, and believeth on him that sent me, hath everlasting life, and shall not come into condemnation (judgement); but is passed from death unto life" (John 5:24).

Such is the God of the Bible, unknown to the Greeks in the times of ignorance, but now made known to all men in the resurrection of Christ and in the preaching of the gospel. Thus, philosophy and human reasoning cannot meet man's deepest need. Forgiveness of sins, and everlasting life, are to be found solely in the risen Lord. This was the lesson for the men of Athens. The God who was unknown had now declared Himself, and was commanding all men everywhere to repent. We shall presently return to this subject to consider further the stunning similarities between Epicurean atheism, Stoic pantheism, and modern-day forms of unbelief.

Idolatry at Ephesus
We have already noted the presence of the occult in Ephesus. Many who had practised the black arts had turned to the Lord, and had made a bonfire of their books. The people who had believed in Christ were cutting off all contact with the temple and its goddess. However, there were others in Ephesus who had a vested interest in goddess worship, and there "arose no small stir about that way" (Acts 19:23). The opposition to the gospel on this occasion came from a guild of silversmiths who specialised in making silver shrines of Diana, a business activity that obviously paid very well. When the silversmiths perceived that Christianity was a threat to their lucrative trade they united in their opposition to Paul and his message.

The leader and spokesman for the silversmiths was an expert agitator named Demetrius. Calling a meeting of the craftsmen, he very cleverly provoked his fellow workers by appealing to their commercial interests and religious pride. Demetrius had three points to make. First, the craft by which they earned their living was under threat from Paul. That was more than enough to have their undivided attention. Second, he claimed that not only in Ephesus but also in almost all Asia, Paul was saying that gods made with hands were not true gods at all. Third, with the masterstroke of a consummate politician, Demetrius predicted that Ephesus would soon lose its position as the world centre of Diana worship. Her temple would be despised, and her magnificence would be destroyed. Demetrius would not be the last to link livelihood to religion and national pride. To be a loyal Ephesian, one had to be a devoted worshipper of the goddess Diana. To become a follower of Christ was to betray their craft, their city, and their national religion.

Demetrius was not appealing to truth, but to a combination of commercial interests, racial pride and religious prejudice. His speech was like a lightning rod that electrified the city. The silversmiths began to chant, "Great is Diana of the Ephesians" and soon the whole population was in uproar. Base bigotry had taken over. The mob caught two of Paul's travelling companions, Gaius and Aristarchus (both Macedonians), and dragged them into the large open-air theatre. Paul wanted to follow them into the theatre but the other believers dissuaded him. Meanwhile, the hostile crowd in the theatre was becoming more and more frenzied and confused.

Among the mob in the theatre was a group of Jews who put forward a man named Alexander to explain their position. But on realising that Alexander was a Jew, the mob did not let him speak, but chanted in unison for two hours "Great is Diana of the Ephesians" (Eph 19:34). Eventually the Town Clerk intervened and tried to restore some semblance of order, addressing the people as "Men of Ephesus". His words to the crowd are most illuminating. He reassured them of the unassailable truth that the city of Ephesus was temple keeper to both the great goddess Diana, and the sacred stone that fell from Jupiter. The Town Clerk considered that such facts were self-evidently true and beyond dispute. On that ground, he appealed to the crowd for quietness and order. The 'image' or sacred stone was possibly a meteorite that had fallen near Ephesus. The stone was venerated by the people as a gift from the god Jupiter. The Ephesians put a lot of faith in that stone, as it seemed to validate their goddess worship.[4]

There is a very practical lesson to be learnt from the words of the town clerk as he appealed to the rioters: "For ye have brought hither these men, which are neither robbers of churches,

---

[4] It is sadly ironic that in more recent times, men once again put faith in a piece of rock, the meteorite ALH84011, which purportedly came from Mars. The meteorite contains nanocrystals that some scientists had hailed as fossil evidence of life on Mars. The Press and Media were swift to announce 'game, set and match' for the theory of evolution. Many other scientists, however, were unconvinced and believed that the prismatic magnetite crystals were not biogenic. Their caution proved to be well justified. It would be a foolish mistake, just as it was in Ephesus, to put one's faith in a stone!

nor yet blasphemers of your goddess" (Acts 19:37). In other words, the Christians had never plundered temples nor interfered with them in any way, nor had they ever blasphemed or defamed their goddess. What a lesson for Christians today! It is not our business to interfere with the property of others, nor ought we ever to ridicule or mock in an insulting way the religious beliefs of others. To point out error to men is one thing; to insult and provoke them is quite another. The brief of the Christian is to preach Christ, without recourse to inflammatory language concerning the religious practices of others.[5] Let the dead bury their dead!

Returning to the biblical narrative, we read that the Town Clerk eventually calmed the crowd and dismissed them. He was obviously an intelligent man and was somewhat ashamed of the behaviour of his townspeople. If Demetrius and his friends had a case against the Christians, they should take it to a proper court. Interestingly, both Demetrius and the town clerk used the same type of appeal to make their case. They linked the worship of Diana to the history and culture of Ephesus. That was a very powerful and emotional objection to the gospel. For an Ephesian to become a Christian, he had to break with the proud history of his city, and dissociate himself from the religion of his fathers. The linking of religious belief to national culture and history is still one of the greatest obstacles that the powers of darkness have put in the way of the gospel. However, grace had triumphed in Ephesus. There was a company of Christians meeting in local church testimony, and who were commended by the Lord Jesus with the words: "for my name's sake hast laboured, and hast not fainted" (Rev 2:3). Incredibly, among these Christians in Ephesus, were those who had once been goddess worshippers. Moreover, grace still triumphs in this way today, just as it did in Ephesus all those years ago.

In conclusion, we have seen that the opposition to the gospel

---

[5] On a personal note, having been brought up in Northern Ireland with its divided community, I am very conscious of the need to present the gospel faithfully in a way that will not stumble or insult any member of the community. The Christian, in my view, should be *apolitical* for the sake of the gospel.

in the first century took many different forms. Paul and his companions had to contend with base bigotry from the pagan world of the occult, idolatry, polytheism, pantheism and mythology. They experienced fierce animosity when commercial interests were at stake. Then there were the more sophisticated and intellectual objections in the materialistic philosophies of Greece. However, whether it was occult or philosophy, polytheism or pantheism, Paul preached the gospel as the only message to meet the need of men, whether Jews or Greeks. We quote again the words of Paul to the Corinthians:

"For the preaching of the cross is to them that perish foolishness; but unto us which are saved it is the power of God....For the Jews require a sign, and the Greeks seek after wisdom: *but we preach Christ crucified*, unto the Jews a stumbling block, and unto the Greeks foolishness; but unto them which are called, both Jews and Greeks, Christ the power of God, and the wisdom of God" (1 Cor 1:18-24).

CHAPTER 4

The Gospel and the 'Modern' World

Should Christianity be relegated to museums? The ideas of sin, forgiveness, and eternal life - are they simply outmoded concepts from the past? Do they need to be reinterpreted for the modern scientific age? Or, on the other hand, is the original gospel message as preached by Paul, as true and vital today as it was in the first century? These are some of the questions that we shall address in this chapter.

In some ways, the world of today is a very different place to the world of Nero. High-tech weapons and smart missiles have changed the methods of warfare beyond all recognition, while science and technology have revolutionised the ways in which people communicate and travel. The imperial age has given way to the information age. If the first century was characterised by empire and conquest, the twenty-first century is marked by globalisation and knowledge. New ideas in the ancient world could travel but slowly along Roman roads, whereas new thoughts in today's internet age can be communicated instantly around the world. Yet, even though the technological and intellectual landscape of the world has been transformed in many ways, human nature has not improved. Man's need is just the same as it always has been. Men today have real moral guilt and do need God's forgiveness and salvation.

Although men have made gigantic strides in science and technology, their prevailing philosophies and life-views have changed remarkably little. Indeed, it is astonishing how quickly the Western world has embraced "post-Christian" culture and has reverted to ancient ideas and heresies. This makes it more important than ever to proclaim to our generation, with all the authority of the Word of God, that the gospel is still "the power of God unto salvation to everyone that believeth; to the Jew first, and also to the Greek" (Rom 1:16).

We have already been considering various first century reactions to the preaching of the gospel, as recorded for us chiefly in the Acts of the Apostles. In this chapter, we shall look at the modern counterparts of those early forms of unbelief, and consider again the message of the gospel for our own generation.

Modern Judaism and the Gospel

Two thousand years ago, the nation of Israel rejected Jesus of Nazareth, choosing instead to release a terrorist named Barabbas. It is a striking and sad irony that today Israel is plagued by terrorists. The history of the Jews has been the saddest chronicle in the story of the human race. Not only did that original generation of Jews slay their Messiah, but also every generation since that time has endorsed the decision made by their ancestors. Today a "blindness in part has happened to Israel, until the fulness of the Gentiles be come in" (Rom 11:25).

The Lord Jesus had lamented over Jerusalem with the words: "O Jerusalem, Jerusalem, thou that killest the prophets, and stonest them that are sent unto thee, how often would I have gathered thy children together, even as a hen gathereth her chickens under her wings, and ye would not. Behold, your house is left unto you desolate" (Matt 23:37-38). Nevertheless, we can say emphatically that God has *not* forsaken Israel forever. There will be a day, on the Lord's second advent, when Israel as a nation shall once again be brought into a believing, covenant relationship with God, as evidenced by the Lord's further words "For I say unto you, Ye shall not see me henceforth, till ye shall say, Blessed is he that cometh in the name of the Lord" (v.39).

On His final arrival at Jerusalem, the Lord Jesus looked on the city and was moved to tears. Luke records the incident for us: "And when he was come near, he beheld the city and wept over it, saying, If thou hadst known, even thou, at least in this thy day, the things which belong unto thy peace! but now they are hid from thine eyes. For the days shall come upon thee, that thine enemies shall cast a trench about thee, and compass thee round, and keep thee in on every side, and shall lay thee even with the ground, and thy children within thee; and they shall not leave in thee one stone upon another; because thou knewest not the time of thy visitation" (Luke 19:41-44).

The Lord's prophecy had its terrible fulfilment in AD 70 when the Roman general Titus sacked Jerusalem, massacring a large part of the population and flattening the temple buildings. The temple activities necessarily ceased and have never resumed to this day. The Jewish people were scattered and Israel as a nation ceased to exist until 1948, when it once again became a nation state. Sadly, it is still a Christ-rejecting nation. Today, Israel has no king, no priest, no altar and no sanctuary. Much as they try, it is not possible for modern Jews to keep the law of Moses. The words of Hosea are having their present day fulfilment: "For the children of Israel shall abide many days without a king, and without a prince, and without a sacrifice, and without an image (pillar), without an ephod, and without teraphim" (Hos 3:4).

At this point, it will be profitable to take a backward glance at what original Mosaic Judaism was actually teaching. Much could be said on such a vast subject, but we can discern three key elements in what the law of Moses taught men:

1) *ABOUT GOD* - The law of Moses taught men that God was absolutely holy and righteous. The commandments, the food laws, the priesthood, the offerings, and the feast days all taught that God is uncompromisingly holy and righteous.

2) *ABOUT HUMAN NATURE* - Further, the law of Moses exposed men's sinful condition and taught them that their fallen nature had rendered them totally incapable of keeping the law. The law could tell a man not to covet, but it could not deliver him from coveting. It simply taught men that they were helpless sinners.

3) *ABOUT MAN'S APPROACH TO GOD* - At the heart and centre of the whole Mosaic/Aaronic system was the

substitutionary sacrifice, which was an illustration or type of the saving work of the Lord Jesus Christ in His death and resurrection. The supreme lesson of the law was that fallen sinful men could approach God on the ground of shed blood, and on that ground alone. There was no other way to come. Modern Jews deny the need of shed blood and sacrifice. They argue that shed blood was only one way, among many ways, by which men could approach God. Should you confront a Jew today with the impossibility of their serving God as His covenant people, he will insist that the feast days and observances can be kept without all the prescribed offerings and temple ceremonies. But by arguing so, they ignore the very foundation of their own history as God's covenant people.

When God redeemed Israel out of Egypt, it was on the basis of shed blood (Exod 12). When God entered into covenant relationship with Israel through the mediation of Moses, the covenant was ratified by blood being sprinkled on the people (Exod 24). Aaron and his sons were consecrated as priests by the sprinkling of blood (Exod 29). When a Hebrew wished to worship or give thanks, he would do so with burnt offerings and peace offerings (Leviticus 1-3). When a transgressor wanted to put things right with God, he would come with his sin offerings and guilt offerings (Lev 4-6). Burnt offerings were offered every morning and every evening, with extra requirements on Sabbaths and New Moons. The annual feasts had many prescribed offerings. But perhaps the most instructive ceremony underlining the need for shed blood was the Day of Atonement (Lev 16). On that day, the high priest went through the veil into the holiest place on the behalf of the people to make atonement for them by sprinkling blood, both before and on the mercy seat. The high priest could enter the holiest place only on one day per year, and never without blood. In fact, it was because there was a blood sprinkled mercy seat in the holiest place, that God was pleased to dwell among His people for another year.

All of these types of blood shedding have their great Antitype in the death of the Lord Jesus Christ. Peter expressed this truth by saying, "Forasmuch as ye know that ye were not redeemed with corruptible things, as silver and gold...but with the precious blood of Christ, as of a lamb without blemish and without spot" (1 Pet 1:18-19).

The central truth of original Mosaic Judaism may be summed up in the words of Leviticus 17:11, "For the life of the flesh is in the blood: and I have given it to you upon the altar to make an atonement for your souls: for it is the blood that maketh an atonement for the soul." Sadly, modern Judaism has abandoned this truth and is now nothing more than a skeletal parody of original Mosaic Judaism. Even so, God is not finished with the nation of Israel. Paul tells us that "blindness in part is happened to Israel, until the fulness of the Gentiles be come in. And so all Israel shall be saved..." (Rom 11:25,26).

Meanwhile, in this present age, God makes no difference between the Jew and the Gentile. The gospel message for both is "Christ crucified". It may indeed be a stumbling block to Jews and foolishness to Greeks, but there is *no other doctrine.*

Regarding the horrendous crime of crucifying their Messiah, the Jews are in denial to this day. Their rejection of Christ in this twenty-first century generation is just as adamant and extreme as the original rejection by their forefathers. They maintain that 'Jesus' cannot save souls, nor did He rise from the dead. This position is equally true of the different branches of modern Judaism, whether Conservative, Reform, Reconstructionist, or Orthodox. However, one slight difference has emerged in recent times in their attitude to Jesus of Nazareth. For many years, the Jews had regarded Jesus as a sorcerer and imposter, but in more recent times they have included Him in their religious and academic studies. However, this does not mean that they are at last facing up to the question of who Jesus of Nazareth really was. Their interest in Christ, which is only comparative, began around the time when liberal theologians were denying the deity of Christ. H.D. Leuner wrote:

"The figure of Jesus became attractive to Judaism only to the extent that the higher criticism in the liberal Christian theology tended to subordinate traditional orthodox beliefs to modern thought. It is no coincidence that Jewish interest in Jesus occurred at a time when Christian doctrine was toned down and modified. An interpretation of Jesus that stripped him of his deity, explained away his miracles and dissected his words, provided a basis of study quite acceptable to Judaism. It was the time when it became fashionable to question the reliability of the gospel records, to feel uncertain about the resurrection appearances, and to dismiss everything supernatural as pious myth." [6]

Modern Judaism does not require that a person convert to Judaism to achieve salvation. The only requirement for salvation, according to Jews, is to be ethical. That is no better than Islam or Buddhism. Sadly, Israel today has no gospel to preach, and has no good news to share with the Gentiles. They still cannot get around that stumbling block of "Christ crucified".

Christendom and the Gospel

When the apostle Paul was executed for the gospel's sake in about 67 AD, there were already in existence many churches of baptised believers throughout the Roman world. The word 'church' is from the Greek *ekklesia*, which means a called out company or assembly. For example, in Paul's letter to the Romans, he greeted Priscilla, Aquilla, and "the church that is in their house" (Rom 16:5). On writing to the Corinthians, he addressed his opening remarks to "the church of God which is at Corinth" (1 Cor 1:2). Paul's letter to the Galatians was written "unto the churches of Galatia" (Gal 1:2). His letter to the Ephesians was for "the saints which are at Ephesus" (Eph 1:1). Similarly, the letter to the Philippians is addressed to "all the saints in Christ Jesus which are at Philippi, with the bishops (overseers) and deacons" (Phil 1:1). Paul greeted the believers in Thessalonica

---

[6] Leuner, H.D. "Judaism" in *The World's Religions* edited by Sir Norman Anderson (Inter-Varsity Press, 1975) p.85-86.

as the "church of the Thessalonians which is in God the Father and in the Lord Jesus Christ" (1 Thess 1:1).

What was it that all of these churches had in common? Who were the members, and on what ground did they gather as a church? In other words, what constituted a New Testament church? We can discern from the Scriptures the distinguishing features of a first century local church:

- Each church gathered and met in the Name of the Lord Jesus Christ. His promised presence in such a company was the ground and doctrine of their gathering (Mat 18:20). Denominationalism, in the modern sense of the term, would have been unknown.
- All the members were believers (Acts 2:41).
- All the believers had been baptised by immersion in water, following their profession of faith in Christ (Acts 2:41).
- There were only two ordinances or 'ceremonies' practised by each church or assembly - the baptism of believers, and the Lord's Supper (Acts 2:41-42). There were no feast days given to the church (Col 2:16-17).
- The members assembled together on the first day of each week for the "Breaking of Bread" meeting (Acts 20:7). They also met regularly for prayer and Bible study.
- There was Spirit-led worship as opposed to a pre-arranged programme (1 Cor 14:26-33)
- Each local church had a plurality of elders/overseers (Acts 20:17), as well as deacons (Acts 6:3).
- Each church was autonomous, with Christ as its only foundation (1 Cor 3:11).
- The churches had fellowship with one another, but had no formal, administrative or organisational link between them.
- The churches engaged in evangelistic activity, i.e. the preaching of the gospel (1 Thes 1:8). They also commended and supported some believers in full time work as missionaries and gospel preachers (Acts 13:1-3).
- When Christians met together as a church, it was custom and practice for the women to remain silent (1 Cor 14:34) and to cover their heads (1 Cor 11:4-6).

(Interestingly, this was opposite to the practice in Jewish synagogues where the men covered their heads and the women uncovered their heads, while in pagan temples neither men nor women covered their heads.) The audible worship and teaching would have been conducted by the men.

It is vital to see the distinction between the "Church which is his body" and the local churches that met in various geographical locations. Every Christian is a member of the "church which is His body", but every Christian is not necessarily a member of a local church. However, it was (and still is) God's intention that every believer should be part of such a local church. For a believer to despise fellowship with other believers meeting in a local church would have been an abnormal situation according to Scripture. There was no such thing as an independent, stand-alone Christian.

Our chief concern in this book is the doctrine of the gospel. We know that the gospel was being communicated by the local churches to the surrounding regions. For example, Paul was able to write to the Thessalonians: "For from you sounded out the word of the Lord not only in Macedonia and Achaia, but also in every place your faith to God-ward is spread abroad; so that we need not to speak any thing" (1 Thess 1:8). What exactly was the function of the churches in relation to the gospel?

It was the responsibility and ministry of the churches to preach and proclaim the gospel to all. Men and women received personal salvation by trusting in Christ. It is vital to understand that the church neither dispensed nor administered salvation, but simply preached it. It is God who saves, not the church. It is highly inaccurate to say that the church possesses the means of salvation. That is the error of sacramentalism. Nor was there any church ceremony which could confer salvation on a man, woman, or child. Baptism, in the New Testament, was exclusively carried out on those who had first confessed faith in Christ. There is not a shred of evidence to suggest that infants were baptised into Christ, nor even into any covenantal relationship. Salvation did not come by baptism, but by personal faith in Christ. Such was the doctrine of the gospel as held by the New Testament churches.

Soon there was to be serious departure from these fundamental truths. Paul had often warned of the apostasy that should soon creep into the churches after his demise. Speaking to the elders of Ephesus, he said, "For I know this, that after my departing shall grievous wolves enter in among you, not sparing the flock. Also of your own selves shall men arise, speaking perverse things, to draw away disciples after them" (Acts 20:29-30). Similarly, he warned Timothy: "Now the Spirit speaketh expressly, that in the latter times some shall depart from the faith, giving heed to seducing spirits, and doctrines of devils; speaking lies in hypocrisy; having their conscience seared with a hot iron; forbidding to marry, and commanding to abstain from meats..." (1 Tim 4:1-3).

In the course of time the gospel of truth, as preached by the early church, was gradually buried under a growing mountain of error. Instead of preaching the gospel of free grace, a sacramental 'church' began to emerge which claimed it possessed the means of salvation, and had the exclusive right to confer such salvation on others. Salvation was taught to be by baptism, and was administered to infants. A sacrificing priesthood arose which was a 'Christianised' copy of the old Aaronic priesthood. The Lord 's Supper, which had been instituted by the Lord Jesus as a memorial, came to be regarded as a literal sacrifice for sins, repeated every day many times over by ordained priests. The Caesar of Rome had been replaced with a new *pontifex maximus* , a high priest of Christendom. The Biblical truth of salvation by grace alone, through faith in Christ alone, was exchanged for a sacramental and meritorious system of salvation.

This new apostate church drew on many forms of paganism for its doctrines and practices. One example will suffice. We have already observed that in the Greco-Roman world, there were gods for every eventuality in life. The major gods had their own temples and were worshipped in accordance with a set calendar. Christendom copied pagan Rome by replacing the Roman gods with "Christian saints". Thus, if a man wanted to make a safe journey, or reap a good harvest, or have a happy marriage, he need no longer appeal to the old pagan deities but could now pray to an ever-growing "pantheon" of saints. Saints were honoured according to a set calendar, while churches and cathedrals were built in their honour and their relics venerated. Today there are over four thousand patron saints canonised by Christendom, each one supposedly with special spheres of influence.

This one example serves to show how far Christendom has departed from the original teaching of the New Testament. According to the scriptures, *every* believer is a saint. When Paul was writing to the Philippians, he addressed his letter to "all the saints in Christ Jesus which are at Philippi" (Phil 1:1). Again, when writing to the believers in Rome, Paul said, "To all that are in Rome, beloved of God, called saints" (Rom 1:7 *JND*). In other words, every Christian is already a saint by the calling of God on his conversion. The idea of believers striving to attain to a special sainthood, which would be conferred on them by the 'church' after their death, is foreign to scripture.

Although it is not within the scope of this book to give an outline of church history, it is necessary to note how far Christendom was moving from the original New Testament teaching on salvation and church order. The gospel had nearly, but not entirely,[7] vanished out of sight. The Western world had entered the epoch of history which would become known as the "Dark Ages".

Happily, the gospel light began to shine again in the 16th century with the coming of the Reformation. Men began to read the Bible for themselves, and soon realised that what the 'church' taught, and what the Bible taught, were two very different things. The battle cry of the Reformers became *sola scriptura* - "by scripture alone". They rediscovered the truth of the common priesthood of all believers. Concerning salvation, Luther's war cry was *sola fide* - "by faith alone". The Reformers

---

[7] For an account of faithful gospel testimony and church practice through the ages, see *The Pilgrim Church* by E.H. Broadbent.

raised their voices against the prevailing sacramental and meritorious system of salvation. The reaction of the Church of Rome was to persecute those who trusted in Christ alone for salvation, and who dared to read the Bible for themselves. Today there is still an assault on the gospel by sacramental Christendom, but of a subtly different kind. Whereas the old response was that of persecution, the new approach is one of compromise. The stratagem of Balaam of long ago was to blur the distinction between the people of God and the Midianites, between truth and error (Rev 2:14). Similarly, the prevailing ideas today are those of ecumenism and pluralism. Ecumenism has blurred the distinction between grace and sacramentalism as the ground of salvation, while pluralism has eroded the uniqueness and exclusivity of the Lord Jesus Christ as the only Saviour of men. The phenomenon of pluralism rightly belongs to the postmodern era, and we will consider it presently in another chapter.

Ecumenism and the Gospel

Is it wise or scriptural to have joint evangelistic campaigns with those who teach a sacramental and meritorious way of salvation? Some "evangelicals" have demoted the reality of personal salvation to nothing more than an optional extra to their existing state of grace that they allegedly received at their baptism as infants. This is error of the worst kind. In the New Testament, grace is contrasted to three things: debt, works, and law. Let us remind ourselves of these vital truths:

Grace in contrast to debt -

Abraham did not put God in his debt, but received the blessing on the ground of grace through faith: "For what saith the scripture? Abraham believed God, and it was reckoned unto him for righteousness. Now to him that worketh is the reward not reckoned of grace, but of debt. But to him that worketh not, but believeth on him that justifieth the ungodly, his faith is counted for righteousness" (Rom 4:3-5). The lesson is clear - in the matter of salvation, no man can put God in his debt in the sense that God would be contractually obliged to give him salvation as his rightful earnings.

Grace in contrast to works -

Paul insisted that salvation was given as a free gift and not as a reward for works: "For by grace are ye saved through faith; and that not of yourselves: it is the gift of God: not of works, lest any man should boast" (Eph 2:8-9; see also Rom 11:6). In other words, works do not give merit for salvation. There is of course a sense in which we are saved *for* good works, but never *by* good works. We cannot merit salvation. It can only be received on the ground of grace, and on the principle of faith.

Grace in contrast to Law -

No one has a legal entitlement to salvation, nor can any man keep the Law in such sense that God would be legally obligated to save him as a law-keeper. John sets out the contrast: "For the law was given by Moses, but grace and truth came by Jesus Christ" (John 1:17). When certain Jews taught that Gentile believers must be circumcised, and that they must keep the law of Moses, Peter objected and said: "Now therefore why tempt ye God, to put a yoke upon the neck of the disciples, which neither our fathers nor we were able to bear? But we believe that through the grace of our Lord Jesus Christ we shall be saved, even as they" (Acts 15:10-11).

Grace is the free, unmerited, and undeserved favour of God to men. Grace is the ground and principle on which God is dealing with the world today. So much so, Paul says that grace reigns (Rom 5:21). In other words, God in His sovereignty is reigning in grace. We must be careful not to use the word 'sovereignty' as if it were a limitation upon grace. We are in the "day of salvation" when *any* sinner, without distinction or exception, can be reconciled to God on the ground of grace (2 Cor 5:20-6:2). It is true that no one can be saved apart from the Spirit's work, but happily, the Holy Spirit has come so that none need perish. The Lord Jesus said that he would send the Holy

Spirit to convince the *world* of sin, righteousness, and judgement (John 16:8). That means that there is no one in the world outside the scope of God's grace in the gospel. Paul told the elders of Ephesus that he had been commissioned by the Lord Jesus to testify to "the gospel of the grace of God" (Acts 20:24). The Bible-believing Christian must be careful not to have fellowship with anything that would de-throne grace. We cannot allow anyone to add works, merit, or law as a means or help to salvation. The ecumenical movement (*i.e.* the coming together of all "Christian denominations") most certainly interferes with the preaching of the gospel. Paul realised that the truth of the gospel was under serious attack by men who wanted to add works of law to grace. Horrified at this prospect, Paul wrote to the Galatian believers, "But though we, or an angel from heaven, preach any other gospel unto you than that which we have preached unto you, let him be accursed." And as though to re-emphasise this weighty statement, he immediately repeats it: "As we said before, so say I now again, If any man preach any other gospel unto you than that we have received, let him be accursed" (Gal 1:8-9).

Modern Philosophy and the Gospel

Renè Descartes (1596-1650) has the dubious honour of being hailed as the first modern philosopher. Rejecting the idea of divine revelation, Descartes postulated that men could discover truth by the natural light of human reason. This became the leading premise of the eighteenth century movement known as the Enlightenment. Beginning with Descartes, and continuing to Immanuel Kant (1724-1804), the age saw the gradual rejection of belief in the personal transcendent God of scripture. Some still held to a belief in God - but it was the false god of the Deists, not the God of the Bible. In this view, God created the universe and immediately took a back seat. He did not involve Himself in the daily activities of men, nor was He needed by men. The emerging spirit was anti-Christian and freethinking, while rationalism became the new creed. Remarkably, the Epicureanism that Paul had encountered in Athens was resurfacing in seventeenth century Europe!

A very old philosophical argument began to resurface. It was alleged that there was a contradiction involved in the fact of evil on the one hand, and belief in an omnipotent and perfect God on the other. The argument goes something like this:

- Evil and suffering exist in the world.
- If God could stop the suffering but will not, then He cannot be all-good.
- If God would stop the suffering, but cannot, then He cannot be all-powerful.
- Therefore, so the argument goes, the fact of evil proves that a God who is both all-powerful and all-good cannot possibly exist.

Is there an answer to this philosophical challenge? The answer is most definitely *yes*. Every Christian ought to be familiar with the Bible answer to the question of evil. Concerning the existence of evil and suffering in the world, we offer a two part answer:

1) The world as we see it today is not as it came from the hand of God. God originally created a perfect world, but what we see today is a fallen world. Evil and suffering did not always exist, nor did God create evil or suffering. The existence of evil and suffering in the world is a direct result of man's rebellion against God. It was human sin that brought fear, enmity, sorrow, curse, and death into the world. (Gen 3:8-24). What is the reason for natural disasters, such as earthquakes, tsunamis, floods, and volcanoes? Again, because of sin, the very ground is cursed, and nature itself is dysfunctional. Evil and suffering are features of a ruined world.

2) God, in the Person of His Son, has already dealt with the problem of evil and suffering. The sin question has been eternally settled on Golgotha's cross, where the Lord Jesus put away sin (Heb 9:26); destroyed the works of the devil (1 John 3:8); and destroyed him that had the power of death, that is,

the devil (Heb 2:14). The last enemy to be destroyed will be death itself (1 Cor 15:26). In heaven, there will be no more death, sorrow, crying, pain, or curse (Rev 21:4; 22:3). The work of Christ on the cross has seen to that. Meanwhile, why does God allow a suffering world to continue in its evil course? The Bible answer is that God is "not willing that any should perish, but that all should come to repentance" (2 Pet 3:9). In other words, the day of grace is running its course so that greater and greater numbers of people will come to faith in Christ, including you and me. Further, God in a future day will deal with this world in judgement. Until that day, judgement is on hold while God deals with the world in grace.

David Gooding, commenting on the problem of evil, had this to say about Peter's reference to Psalm 110:1 in Acts Chapter 2: "It was never part of God's programme that the Messiah should proceed, immediately upon his exaltation, to stamp out evil. The invitation was, "Sit at my right hand *until* I make your enemies your footstool." There was to be an interval between his exaltation and the subjugation of his enemies, during which he would be seated at God's right hand, awaiting the time of his second coming. Only then would his enemies be made the footstool of his feet...What if there had been no interval, and he had proceeded at once to stamp out evil? We are, Peter pointed out, already in the last days of this present age. The cosmic convulsions will occur soon enough, to be followed by the great and resplendent day of the Lord, and the dawning of the messianic age to come. But thank God for the present interval."[8]

The question of evil is therefore answered fully by the cross of Christ. God's power and goodness have not been compromised by the problem of evil, but rather have been magnified in Christ by His finished work on the cross. Because of Calvary, God is currently saving sinners, and will one day abolish from His creation every last trace of death and evil. It is highly interesting to note that this philosophical objection is not a modern or recent challenge to Christianity, but is an ancient

---

[8] Gooding, David *True to the Faith* (Hodder & Stoughton, 1990) p.66.

argument; first formulated by Epicurus, the founding father of Epicureanism.[9] It is a very old virus indeed!

The Enlightenment, with its method of doubt, produced critical thinkers who believed in the power of unaided human reason. A new mathematical-mechanistic approach was applied to all fields of knowledge, and it was only a matter of time until the new critical method was applied to theology. If modern philosophy started with Descartes, modern theology is said to have begun with Friedrich Schleiermacher (1768-1834). Refusing to accept the Bible as "a narrative of divine interventions and a collection of divine utterances"[10], Schleiemacher considered that the Bible was not to be taken seriously in every detail, but was merely a record of religious experience. The miracles were to be regarded as symbols rather than factual reports. The Genesis account of the fall of Adam and Eve was not to be considered biographical, but as a "symbolic account of a universal element in human experience".[11] And, according to Schleiermacher, 'Jesus' was the revelation of God only in the sense of initiating a "new and wholesome form of self-consciousness".

Thus began the era of 'modernism' in the religious world. With an eye on the findings of natural science, the liberals claimed that it was necessary to revise the gospel in a way that would appeal to modern men. The implications of this new approach were devastating for faith and doctrine. It was not long until churchgoers were being told by their ministers that the Bible contained errors, myths and exaggerations. The foundations had been severely shaken, with congregations dividing over the nature of Biblical truth. Liberal Protestantism had become the new enemy of the gospel.

The new breed of textual critics, especially those from Germany, was critically appraising the Bible on the assumption

---

[9] Hunnex, Milton D. *Chronological and Thematic Charts of Philosophies and Philosophers* (Zondervan, Grand Rapids, 1986) p.35.

[10] Brown, Colin *Philosophy and the Christian Faith* (Inter-varsity Press, Reprint 1974) p.110.

[11] Galloway, Alan D. "Schleiermacher" in *The History of Christian Theology* Vol 1 *The Science of Theology* Ed. Paul Avis (Marshall Pickering, 1986) p.247.

that it was merely an imperfect collection of ordinary human writings. Everything was challenged and doubted, from authorship to historical accuracy. In the Old Testament, the first five books were said to have been written, not by Moses, but by many writers. The content of Genesis was dismissed as legend. Books, which clearly were written before the Babylonian exile, were attributed to unknown authors after the exile, who allegedly wrote the narratives with the benefit of hindsight. The book of Isaiah was said to be not one book, but at least two books. It was claimed that the book of Daniel was not written in the period it describes. In the New Testament, the four gospels were said to have been written long after the reported events, by which time the original stories had grown into fables of epic proportions. The fourth Gospel was said to be radically different from the first three Gospels, and could not be considered reliable. The virgin birth, the miracles, the resurrection and ascension were all dismissed as myth. The authorship of some of Paul's letters was also challenged, while Paul himself was said to be the falsifier of the "original teachings of Jesus", and the inventor of his own version of corrupted Christianity.

Not surprisingly, the churches which adopted this liberal theology experienced a relentless decline in their membership. By teaching that the Bible contained all kinds of mistakes, the liberals were effectively giving their congregations notice to quit! The tools and methods of textual criticism employed by modernist scholars have been carried over wholesale into the critical apparatus of the postmodern scholars.

How then should the believer respond to this assault on the Bible and on the Person of Christ? We shall suggest scriptural answers in the three areas of: (1) The Inspiration of the Scriptures; (2) The Person of Christ; and (3) The Apostleship of Paul.

1) The Inspiration of Scripture

It is not my intention to discuss the reliability of the Greek and Hebrew manuscripts on which our Bible is based. The subject of Textual Criticism is a specialist field and has been adequately addressed by many eminent conservative scholars. What I want to highlight is the *internal* evidence[12] for the inerrancy and inspiration of the Bible, a profitable and edifying study that can readily be grasped by every believer. We contend that the liberal position is not compatible with true faith. We appeal primarily, as Christians, to the words of the Lord Jesus as conclusive proof of inspiration.

The Lord Jesus clearly considered the characters of the Old Testament to be real people, referring by name to Abel, Noah, Lot, Abraham, Isaac, Jacob, Moses, David, Abiathar, Solomon, Elijah, Elisha, Naaman, Isaiah, Daniel, Zecharias, Barachias and Jonah. Further, the Lord regarded the events recorded in scripture to be accurate and true history, *e.g.* the creation, the institution of marriage, Noah's flood, the destruction of Sodom and Gomorrah, Moses and the burning bush, Moses and the brass serpent, David's eating of the shewbread, the Queen of Sheba's visit to Solomon, the great fish swallowing Jonah, and the repentance of the city of Nineveh.

The Lord often quoted from the Old Testament, investing it with the authority and inspiration of God Himself. He alluded to many Old Testament books, and quoted directly from at least fourteen of them, *viz.* Genesis, Exodus, Leviticus, Numbers, Deuteronomy, Samuel, Kings, Psalms, Isaiah, Jeremiah, Daniel, Hosea, Zechariah and Malachi. When quoting from the Old Testament, the Lord Jesus variously introduced the scriptures with words such as 'have ye not read', 'have ye not read in the law', 'have ye not read what David did', 'have you not read this scripture', 'David himself said by the Holy Ghost', 'well hath Isaiah prophesied', 'it is written in the prophets', and 'spoken of by Daniel the prophet'.

The Lord's words indicate that He put the highest estimate on the Old Testament writings, holding them to be the authoritative and inspired word of God. Further, the Lord

---

[12] For an excellent treatment of the external evidence see Josh McDowell *The New Evidence that Demands a Verdict* and F.F. Bruce *The Books and the Parchments*.

taught men that the scriptures cannot be broken (John 10:35), that they will never pass away (Matt 24:35), and that they must be fulfilled (Lu 24:44). The narratives recorded were not legend, but real historical events, and the persons named were not mythical, but actual people. As the following quotation will show, the Lord did not teach that some scriptures were inspired, nor that the scriptures simply contained truth, but rather that *every word* of the Bible was inspired by God: "Think not that I am come to destroy the law, or the prophets: I am not come to destroy, but to fulfil. For verily I say unto you, Till heaven and earth pass, one jot or one tittle shall in no wise pass from the law, till all be fulfilled. Whosoever therefore shall break one of these least commandments, and shall teach men so, he shall be called the least in the kingdom of heaven: but whosoever shall do and teach them, the same shall be called great in the kingdom of heaven" (Mat 5:17-19).

The liberal approach to scripture, with its underlying unbelief, is not exclusive to the modern age. The Lord Jesus came up against the same critical spirit in the Sadducees, who like modern 'Enlightenment' men, did not believe in resurrection, angel or spirit (Acts 23:8). On one occasion, they challenged the Lord with a hypothetical puzzle, which at first sight appeared to discredit the idea of resurrection as something hopelessly problematic. The Lord's answer is most illuminating. He told the Sadducees: "Ye do err, not knowing the scriptures, nor the power of God" (Matt 22:29). Exactly the same answer can be given today to those of the modern rationalistic mind, for they most certainly err, knowing neither the scriptures, nor the power of God!

The inspiration and truth of scripture is not only proven by the Lord's words as recorded in the four Gospels, but is also attested to in the other writings of the New Testament. Paul told Timothy that "all scripture is given by inspiration of God" (2 Tim 3:16). Peter said that the word of God lives and abides forever (1 Pet 1:23), and that the prophetic scriptures came, not by the will of man, but by holy men of God who spoke as "they were moved by the Holy Ghost" (2 Pet 1:19-21).

A further word is necessary as to the integrity of the New Testament writers. Assuming that the writings are genuine productions of the men whose names they bear, can we actually believe the authors? Are Matthew, Mark, Luke, John, Paul, Peter and Jude the kind of men you could trust? Were they given to exaggeration? Did their memories play tricks on them with the passing of time?

Let us, for a moment, cross-examine Peter and John about some of their more incredible claims, and judge for ourselves if they sound like reliable witnesses. Theoretically, there can be three possible outcomes to our line of enquiry. First, one possibility is that the disciples were self-deluded and their claims were largely myth. Second, there is the theoretical possibility that the disciples had deliberately conspired to deceive and mislead. The third possibility is that they really had seen and heard the reported events, exactly as described. In other words, they were telling the truth.

The Gospels record that on the mount of transfiguration, Peter, James and John saw the face of the Lord Jesus shine as the sun, and heard a voice which said: "This is my beloved Son, in whom I am well pleased; hear ye him" (Matt 17:5). Approaching this story as objective investigators, we must ask how reliable the witnesses are. Is the story true, or is it a kind of folk myth that grew in the minds of the disciples with the passage of time? Or worse, could there have been a conspiracy to invent a fable?

Let us put Peter in the witness box and listen to him reflect on the incident in later life: "For we have not followed cunningly devised fables, when we made known unto you the power and coming of our Lord Jesus Christ, but were *eyewitnesses* of his majesty. For he received from God the Father honour and glory, when there came such a voice to him from the excellent glory, This is my beloved Son, in whom I am well pleased. And this voice which came from heaven *we heard*, when we were with him in the holy mount" (2 Pet 1:16-18). Does this sound like the ramblings of a deluded and unreliable witness, or does it have an overwhelming ring of truth? The answer is obvious - Peter is an excellent and trustworthy witness. He claims that he was an *eyewitness* to the Lord's glory, and that he had *heard* the voice from heaven. There is absolutely no ground for doubting Peter's integrity as a witness.

Having listened to Peter's testimony, let us now turn to John. As he reflected on the life and times of the Saviour, had John become confused about what he had actually seen and heard? Was he confusing facts with fantasy as he grew older? We shall allow John to speak for himself: "That which was from the beginning, which we have heard, which we have seen with our eyes, which we have looked upon, and our hands have handled, of the Word of life; (for the life was manifested, and we have seen it, and bear witness, and shew unto you that eternal life, which was with the Father, and was manifested unto us) that which we have seen and heard declare we unto you, that ye also may have fellowship with us: and truly our fellowship is with the Father, and with his Son Jesus Christ. And these things write we unto you, that your joy may be full" (1 John 1:1-4). Do these words sound like the product of a confused and over-active memory, or do they sound like the accurate and true testimony of a reliable eyewitness? John claims to have heard, seen and handled the Word of life. Again, in the opening chapter of his Gospel, John wrote: "and we beheld his glory, the glory as of the only begotten of the Father" (John 1:14). These are not the words of a dreamer or deceiver, but the thoughtful and accurate testimony of an honest man.

The reader must decide if the Bible writers were reliable and trustworthy witnesses. It was the Lord Jesus Himself who appointed the apostles that they should be witnesses to Him throughout the world (Acts 1:8). Can we believe them? Yes, we can have absolute confidence in our Bible, knowing that "all scripture is given by inspiration of God" (2 Tim 3:16). We can and must present the Bible to modern men as the infallible, inerrant, true, and inspired word of God. In fact, in a changing and uncertain world, the Bible is the only dependable and unchanging reference point, the revealed mind of God to man. The Christian should be fully aware that liberal theology is the modern-day leaven of the Sadducees, an evil that destroys faith and empties churches.

Luke, the physician, wrote his gospel for the benefit of a man named Theophilus. Luke was not one of the twelve, nor was he an apostle. In fact, he was not even a Jew. Yet he wrote two books in the New Testament: the gospel that bears his name, and the Acts of the Apostles. Why should we believe Luke? Was he a reliable recorder of the events of those times? We shall allow Luke to declare his own credentials: "Forasmuch as many have taken in hand to set forth in order a declaration of those things which are most surely believed among us, even as they delivered them unto us, which *from the beginning were eyewitnesses*, and ministers of the word; it seemed good to me also, having had perfect (accurate) understanding of all things from the very first, to write unto thee in order, most excellent Theophilus, that thou mightest know the certainty of those things, wherein thou hast been instructed" (Luke 1:1-4). Luke had been following events closely, and had recorded many things based on eyewitness accounts. He wrote with the accuracy of a historian, taking care to place events in the timescale of Jewish and Roman history. For example, in Luke 1:5, he records that Zecharias was a priest of the course of Abia "in the days of Herod, the king of Judea". Similarly, Joseph's journey to Bethlehem was at the time of the decree of Caesar Augustus, when Cyrenius was governor of Syria (Luke 2:1-2). The ministry of John the Baptist began in the fifteenth year of Tiberius Caesar, when Pontius Pilate was governor of Judea, and Herod was tetrarch of Galilee, and his brother Philip tetrarch of Ituraea and Trachonitus, and Lysanias was tetrarch of Abilene. Having located the event in the context of Roman history, Luke then brings in a Jewish dimension, adding that it was during the high priesthood of Annas and Caiaphas (Luke 3:1-2).

Does this sound like the language of myth? Absolutely not! Luke has written, under the guidance of the Holy Spirit, a remarkable record of events concerning the ministry of the

Lord Jesus, pinpointing geographical locations (especially in the Acts) and establishing the events within Roman and Jewish time frames. Luke's stated reason for writing the gospel was that Theophilus might know the *certainty* of the things of which he had been informed. The Holy Spirit has been pleased to ensure that we too, in the twenty-first century, can know the truth and certainty of the events we read about in our Bible.

2) The Person of Christ

The drastic implications of the new critical approach to scripture soon became clear. The Lord Jesus was deemed to be a mere man, just like any other man. His knowledge was said to be influenced and limited by the prevailing ideas of the times. His deity and eternal pre-existence were flatly denied as later Pauline invention. The modern scholars assured us that He was not virgin-born, neither did He perform miracles, nor was His death sin atoning, nor did He rise from the dead. He was simply a man who had greater spiritual insights than His contemporaries, who died an untimely martyr's death, and whose body had long since returned to dust. Meanwhile, He had left an example of how evil can be overcome with good, and how adversity can be met with courage. His resurrection was to be understood, not in physical terms, but in spiritual terms, showing how a man can rise above his circumstances. Such was the 'Jesus' of modernism.

Theologians such as Rudolf Bultmann (1884-1976) spoke of demythologising the New Testament and repackaging it in a way acceptable to the modern scientific mind. Bultmann proposed that it was not necessary to believe in the "historical Jesus" of the gospels, but rather in the "transcendent Christ" as proclaimed by the church, by which we can have better self-understanding. It is not the "historical Jesus" who matters, but the *idea* of Jesus as proclaimed by the church. Commenting on the claim by Bultmann and the liberals to be able to discern the New Testament narratives as myth,

C.S.Lewis scathingly remarked: "They claim to see fern-seed and can't see an elephant ten yards away in broad daylight."[13]

The leading premise of the liberal gospel is that 'Jesus' is one of us, and we can be very proud of the spiritual resources residing in each human breast. However, this is a false gospel that inflates man, telling him that he can realize his own spiritual potential, without the need for redemption. This false 'Jesus' is powerless to save anybody.

The question arises whether this modernist view of Christ is a new phenomenon, or is merely a very old lie that has resurfaced in modern times. Once again, we discover that these heresies go right back to Bible times. The Lord Jesus warned the disciples "Take heed lest any man deceive you: for many shall come in my name, saying, I am Christ; and shall deceive many" (Mk 13:5-6). Just as there shall be deceivers who will claim to be Christ in the literal and personal sense, so now there are those who preach "another Jesus" (2 Cor 11:4). John asks the rhetorical question: "Who is a liar but he that denieth that Jesus is the Christ? He is antichrist, that denieth the Father and the Son" (1 John 2:22). Again, John continues his warning by saying: "Beloved, believe not every spirit, but try the spirits whether they are of God: because many false prophets are gone out into the world. Hereby know ye the Spirit of God: every spirit that confesseth not that Jesus Christ is come in the flesh is not of God: and this is that spirit of antichrist, whereof ye have heard that it should come; and even now already is it in the world" (1 John 4:1-3).

How should the believer respond to the modern claim that the "historical Jesus" does not matter, and that we can believe in 'Jesus' without believing the Gospel records? Paul answers the question for us by defining the content of the gospel: "Moreover, brethren, I declare unto you the gospel which I preached unto you...For I delivered unto you first of all that which I received, how that Christ died for our sins according to

---

[13] Lewis C.S. *Fern-seed and Elephants* (Collins Fount Paperback, 1975) p.111.

the scriptures; and that he was buried, and that he rose again the third day according to the scriptures" (1 Cor 15:1-4). In other words, His death was sin atoning, His burial was literal, and His resurrection was physical. Further, there were many reliable eyewitnesses to His resurrection appearances. The gospel is a message rooted in real, historical events experienced by our Lord Jesus Christ. Any preacher who tells us differently is a "false teacher," and the Christ he proclaims is "another Jesus."

When the Saviour asked His disciples "Whom do men say that I am? " (Mat 16:13), the disciples replied that some said John the Baptist, others Elijah, others Jeremiah, and yet others one of the prophets. The Lord then turned the question directly on the disciples and enquired: "But whom say ye that I am?" How should we answer the question in this twenty-first century scientific age? He is indeed the true "historical Jesus" of scripture, even our Lord Jesus Christ. It is vital that we do not compromise one iota on this most fundamental of truths, and that we answer believingly with Peter: "Thou art the Christ, the Son of the living God" (Mat 16:16).

3) The Apostleship of Paul

No apostle is held in greater derision and contempt by unbelievers than Paul. The liberal school taught that 'Jesus' had simply wanted to play an accepted role within Judaism, and that it was Paul who was the inventor of Christianity. He did so by "creating the myth of an atoning death of a divine being". Some went so far as to say that Paul derived this idea "from Hellenistic sources, chiefly by a fusion of concepts taken from Gnosticism and concepts taken from the mystery religions, particularly from that of Attis". Liberal Protestantism accused Paul of being, at best, the Helleniser of Christianity, and at worst, the deliberate falsifier of the original Christianity of Jesus, and the inventor of his own religion. Christianity was best expressed in the Sermon on the Mount, so they said, and Paul had distorted it beyond recognition.

Why has Paul been the victim of such virulent character

assassination? The answer to that question is that the liberals and modernists had an agenda. The two leading presuppositions which they brought to their interpretation of scripture were   first, that the Bible was not the inspired and inerrant word of God, and second, that 'Jesus' was not the Son of God. For the liberals, Christ was a very good man, but nothing more. It was His ethical teaching that mattered, not His deity. They wanted Christianity without Christ. The greatest obstacle to this aim was obviously the teaching contained in Paul's epistles. How was one to accommodate the epistles of Paul, and at the same time claim that Christ's deity was simply a romantic myth?

There was only one answer, and that was to portray Paul as a mythmaker and falsifier. To discredit Paul would be to discredit the doctrine. Yet again, we might ask ourselves whether this denigration of Paul is a modern trend resulting from the "assured results of modern scholarship", or is something that had already begun when Paul was alive. The answer, not surprisingly, is that Paul endured in his own lifetime a campaign of hate, lies and innuendo. His character, his doctrine, and his apostolic authority all came under attack. Here are some of the accusations made against Paul by his contemporaries:

• *Accused by Gentiles of subverting Roman law*:

"These men, being Jews, do exceedingly trouble our city, and teach customs, which are not lawful for us to receive, neither to observe, being Romans" (Acts 16:20-21).

• *Accused by Jews of subverting Roman law*:

"These that have turned the world upside down are come hither also; whom Jason hath received: and these all do contrary to the decrees of Caesar, saying that there is another king, one Jesus" (Acts 17:6-7).

• *Accused by Jews of subverting the law of Moses*:

"And when Gallio was the deputy of Achaia, the Jews made insurrection with one accord against Paul, and brought him to the judgment seat, saying, This fellow persuadeth men to worship God contrary to the law" (Acts 18:12-13).

• *Accused by Gentiles of subverting ethnic religion:*

"Moreover ye see and hear, that not alone at Ephesus, but almost throughout all Asia, this Paul hath persuaded and turned away much people, saying that they be no gods, which are made with hands: so that not only this our craft is in danger to be set at nought; but also that the temple of the great goddess Diana should be despised, and her magnificence should be destroyed, whom all Asia and the world worshippeth" (Acts 19:26-27).

• *Accused by Asian Jews of profaning the temple:*

"Men of Israel, help: This is the man, that teaches all men every where against the people, and the law, and this place: and further brought Greeks also into the temple, and hath polluted this holy place" (Acts 21:28).

• *Accused by the chief captain, Claudius Lysias, of being an Egyptian terrorist:*

"Art thou not that Egyptian, which before these days madest an uproar, and leddest out into the wilderness four thousand men that were murderers?" (Acts 21:38).

• *Accused by the Jews of being unfit to live:*

"Away with such a fellow from the earth: for it is not fit that he should live" (Acts 22:22).

• *Accused by the Jews of fomenting sedition among Jews:*

"For we have found this man a pestilent fellow, and a mover of sedition among all the Jews throughout the world, and a ringleader of the sect of the Nazarenes: who hath also gone about to profane the temple" (Acts 24:5-6).

• *Accused by Festus of being mad:*

"Paul, thou art beside thyself; much learning doth make thee mad" (Acts 27:24).

• *Accused by Maltese natives of being an escaped murderer:*

"No doubt this man is a murderer, whom, though he hath escaped the sea, yet vengeance suffered not to live" (Acts 28:4).

• *Accused by some of deliberately promoting evil:*

And not rather, (as we be slanderously reported, and as some affirm that we say,) Let us do evil, that good may come?" (Rom 3:8).

- *Accused by Pharisee believers of preaching an incomplete gospel*:

"But there rose up certain of the sect of the Pharisees which believed, saying, That it was needful to circumcise them, and to command them to keep the law of Moses" (Acts 15:5).

- *Accused by believers of abusing his apostleship*:

"If I be not an apostle unto others, yet doubtless I am to you: for the seal of mine apostleship are ye in the Lord. Mine answer to them that do examine me is this, Have we not power to eat and to drink?" (1 Cor 9:2-4).

- *Accused by some believers of making up his own commandments*:

"If any man think himself to be a prophet, or spiritual, let him acknowledge that the things that I write unto you are the commandments of the Lord" (1 Cor 14:37).

- *Accused by some believers of walking according to the flesh*:

"But I beseech you, that I may not be bold when I am present with that confidence, wherewith I think to be bold against some, which think of us as if we walked according to the flesh. For though we live in the flesh, we do not war after the flesh" (2 Cor 10:2-3).

- *Accused by some believers of having a weak presence and contemptible speech*:

"For his letters, say they, are weighty and powerful; but his bodily presence is weak, and his speech contemptible" (2 Cor 10:10).

- *Accused by some believers of having an inferior apostleship*:

"For if he that cometh preacheth another Jesus, whom we have not preached, or if ye receive another spirit, which ye have not received, or another gospel, which ye have not accepted, ye might well bear with him. For I suppose I was not a whit behind the very chiefest apostles." (2 Cor 11:4-5). "I am become a fool in glorying; ye have compelled me: for I ought to have been commended of you: for in nothing am I behind the very chiefest apostles, though I be nothing. Truly the signs of an apostle were wrought among you in all patience, in signs, and wonders, and mighty deeds (2 Cor 12:11-12).

• *Accused by some believers of guile in financially exploiting the Christians*:

"And I will very gladly spend and be spent for you; though the more abundantly I love you, the less I be loved. But be it so, I did not burden you: nevertheless, being crafty, I caught you with guile" (2 Cor 12:15-16).

• *Accused by some of having written a letter saying that the day of the Lord had already arrived*:

"Now we beseech you, brethren, by the coming of our Lord Jesus Christ, and by our gathering together unto him, that ye be not soon shaken in mind, or be troubled, neither by spirit, nor by word, nor by letter as from us, as that the day of the Lord (*ESV*) is at hand" (2 Thess 2:1-2).

Paul, answering for himself against the charges from unbelieving Jews and Gentiles, said "Neither against the law of the Jews, neither against the temple, nor yet against Caesar, have I offended any thing at all" (Acts 25:8). It was bad enough for Paul to have suffered such slander from unbelievers, but it must have been even more hurtful for him to have been misrepresented by fellow believers. Regarding the charge of preaching an incomplete gospel, Paul gave an extended answer in his letter to the Galatians. He reminded his readers that he had not received the gospel from man: "But I certify you, brethren, that the gospel which was preached of me is not after man. For I neither received it of man, neither was I taught it, but by the *revelation of Jesus Christ*" (Gal 1:11-12).

Regarding the attacks on his apostleship and conduct, Paul gave a detailed defence in his second letter to the Corinthians. There were many of Paul's contemporaries who wished to discredit his doctrine, authority and motives. And so it is today. In modern times, there has been no greater enemy of Paul than liberal Protestantism. It is profoundly wrong to dismiss some aspect of truth by claiming, "it was only Paul who said that". It is vital to understand that the inspired letters of Paul in our New Testament carry all the authority of our Lord Jesus Christ. One must read them, not like a modern critic in unbelief, but like Peter, who wrote: "And account that the longsuffering of our Lord is salvation; even as our beloved brother Paul also according to the wisdom given unto him hath written unto you; as also in all his epistles, speaking in them of these things; in which are some things hard to be understood, which they that are unlearned and unstable wrest, as they do also *the other scriptures*, unto their own destruction" (2 Pet 3:15-16).

Conclusion

The modernists, in their unbelief, had emptied the gospel of its power and truth, just as the Sadducees had done in their day. Schleiermacher was followed by a succession of unbelieving critics, each eager to destroy faith in the Bible. Christianity had become, in their thinking, nothing more than a 'true or helpful myth'. The growing army of theologians who wrote in sympathy with liberal ideas included such names as Hegel, Strauss, Feuerbach, Wellhausen, Schweitzer, Harnock, Bultmann and Tillich. They each added their potion of poison, until there was nothing left but 'death in the pot'.

One theologian who appeared to take a stand against liberalism was the celebrated Karl Barth (1886-1968). However, he advocated a return, not to the old orthodoxy, but to *neo*-orthodoxy. He claimed that modern theology would need to change from being man-centred to being God-centred. That sounds appealing, but unfortunately his approach to textual criticism was liberal, and his view of salvation was universalist. Barth has rightly been referred to as an "anti-modern modernist".[14] One quotation will suffice to show how far Barth had departed from the gospel of scripture: "Man is no longer regarded by God as a sinner. Whatever he may be, whatever there is to be said of him, whatever he has to reproach himself with, God no longer takes him seriously as a sinner. He has died to sin; there on the cross of Golgotha....We are no longer addressed and regarded by God as sinners....We are acquitted

---

[14] Mohler, R. Albert Jr. "The Integrity of the Evangelical Tradition and the Challenge of the Postmodern Paradigm" in *The Challenge of Postmodernism* Ed David S. Dockery (Victor Books, 1995) p.76.

gratis, *sola gratia*, by God's own entering in for us."[15] In other words, Barth is saying that God does not see some people as 'in Christ' and others as 'out of Christ', but that God now looks upon all men as forgiven in Jesus Christ. But that is the most appalling error, and goes against the plain message of the gospel. It is 'another gospel' which lulls men into a false sense of security. In fact, it reminds one of the serpent's original lie in the garden "Ye shall not surely die" (Gen 3:4).

We need go no further in our consideration of liberal Protestantism. It has been necessary to go over this old ground another time, seeing that many of the assumptions of modernism have been accepted as a 'given' by the postmodern school. I trust it has served to underline the need for keeping to the scriptures, and allowing 'no other doctrine'.

---

15 Barth, Karl *Dogmatics in Outline* (New York: Philosophical Library), 1949, p.121,120 [http://www.perichoresis.org/karl_barth.htm] 14 July 2003.

CHAPTER 5

The Question of Origins

Liberal theology, coming out of Enlightenment philosophy, proved to be a ferocious and destructive enemy of faith. But yet another monster was waiting in the wings that would do untold harm to men's confidence in the Bible. In 1859, Charles Darwin published *The Origin of Species by Means of Natural Selection*. It was, in the diabolical scheme of things, a lie whose time had come.

The new theory of evolution seemingly offered a naturalistic explanation for the origin of life, and so the Genesis account of creation could be summarily dismissed as legend. According to Darwin and his followers, all biological life had a common ancestry that had evolved from simple organisms into increasingly more complex life forms by a process of natural selection over long periods of time. Man was no longer regarded as a special creation distinct from animals, but as a kind of higher ape. In other words, he had non-human origins and was simply one animal among other animals. The implications of such a hypothesis for Christianity and the gospel were enormous.

Never was a theory more eagerly embraced by both secular scientists and liberal theologians. The idea of evolution soon permeated all the natural and earth sciences, and much more besides. The concept and term have been adopted by biologists, botanists, astrophysicists, geologists, psychologists, and anthropologists. In the 1940's, the Russian-born American nuclear physicist George Gamow, proposed a big-bang model of the universe that purported to account for the origin of the entire cosmos. The universe, according to this theory, emerged by an explosion about 15 billion years ago from a highly compressed primordial state to an expanding universe. In the course of time, from the first nano-second to billions of years hence, particles formed, galaxies were born, planetary systems came into being, and organic life evolved from non-life. It seemed that origins could now be explained in purely mathematical-mechanistic terms, without the need for a Creator. It looked very much as if science had disproved the Bible - or had it?

Many evolutionists are now claiming that molecular biology provides the most detailed and convincing evidence available for biological evolution. It is argued that the similarities of DNA in different organisms indicate a genetic continuity and common ancestry in all organisms. But is molecular biology as evolution-friendly as is claimed by the textbooks? It is in this very field that some of the greatest problems for evolutionary theory have emerged. Michael Behe, Professor of Biochemistry at Leigh University, has published a devastating challenge to Darwinian evolution. In his book, *Darwin's Black Box,* Behe considers the problem of complexity in several areas of Biochemistry, viz. proteins, blood clotting, cells, immune system, and biosynthesis. Behe states, "Science has made enormous progress in understanding how the chemistry of life works, but the elegance and complexity of biological systems at the molecular level have paralysed science's attempt to explain their origins. There has virtually been no attempt to account for the origin of specific, complex biomolecular systems, much less any progress. Many scientists have gamely asserted that explanations are already in hand, or will be sooner or later, but no support for such assertions can be found in the professional science literature. More importantly, there are compelling reasons - based on the structure of the systems themselves- to think that a Darwinian explanation for the mechanisms of life will forever prove elusive."[16]

---

[16] Behe, Michael J. *Darwin's Black Box - The Biochemical Challenge to Evolution* (Touchstone, NY, 1996) preface.

Another challenge to Darwinian evolution has been made by the British scientist, Dave Swift, who argues the impossibility of obtaining biological macromolecules by chance, even progressively. Swift writes, "Whatever other difficulties there may be, such as gaps in the fossil record, or whatever aspects of evolution may be substantiated, such as morphological change due to the selection and segregation of genes - whatever the other arguments for or against, an overriding factor is that biological macromolecules have proved to be much too complex, much too specific, and much too numerous to be accounted for by the current theory of evolution. It is not just that they are so improbable that they could not possibly have arisen by chance, but there is no evidence that they have acquired their complexity gradually, and no plausible means by which they could do so."[17]

It is interesting to observe the tortuous attempts by scientists to explain the evolution of the most sophisticated of all organs, the human brain. Bruce Lahn, an assistant professor of human genetics at the University of Chicago and an investigator at Howard Hughes Medical Institute, has published results of his research in the journal *Cell*,[18] in which he concludes that humans evolved their cognitive abilities not owing to a few sporadic and accidental mutations - as is the usual way with traits in living things - but rather from an enormous number of mutations in a short period of time, acquired through an intense selection process favouring complex cognitive abilities. Commenting on the fact that human evolution appears to have far outstripped the evolution of other animals, Prof Lahn said, "We've proven that there is a big distinction. Human evolution is, in fact, a privileged process because it involves a large number of mutations in a large number of genes. To accomplish so much in so little evolutionary time - a few tens of millions of

---

[17] Swift, Dave *Evolution under the Microscope - A Scientific Critique of the Theory of Evolution* (Leighton Academic Press, UK, 2002) p.363.
[18] "Accelerated Evolution of Nervous System Genes in the Origin of *Homo sapiens*" by Prof Bruce Lahn *et al*, in the Journal *Cell* Volume 119, Issue 7, 29 December 2004 pp.1027-1040, as reported in *The Guardian*, December 29, 2004.

years - requires a selective process that is perhaps categorically different from the typical processes of acquiring new biological traits." Quite so! These extraordinary conclusions indicate that the theory of evolution has reached breaking point when it comes to proposing mechanisms that could account for the human brain. The normal evolutionary model, that speaks of 'chance mutations over very long periods of time', is being replaced with a model which proposes an 'enormous number of mutations over a short period of time'. We are now being told that that the human brain is the result of 'extraordinarily fast' evolution. For those who have eyes to see it, the theory is imploding.

Is Darwin's theory of evolution a modern scientific theory or simply a very old idea repackaged for the scientific age? We have already noted that the Epicureans believed that the universe was formed by chance collisions of atoms, a phenomenon which eventually led to life and man. There was no purpose and no ultimate meaning to life. Everything happened by blind chance. It all sounds a little like the ideas of Richard Dawkins, who is today's most popular exponent of the 'blind watch maker' philosophy. Commenting on Dawkin's ideas as compared to those of the Epicureans, Dr David Gooding had this to say: "Modern theories of evolution, like those of Dr Richard Dawkins - see, for example, his *The Blind Watchmaker* (London: Longman, 1986) - which stress the effect of *gradual cumulative* development worked on by natural selection, are only more sophisticated versions of this ancient theory. Indeed the theory of evolution itself is not in fact a modern theory, but a very ancient one."[19]

The Bible teaches us that plant life, animal life, and human life were specially created by God, each with their own value, function and purpose. Different kinds of plant life were created from the beginning, each kind with its seed in itself. Similarly, fish, birds and animals were created according to

---

[19] Gooding, David *True to the Faith* (Hodder & Stoughton, London, 1990) Footnote, p.295.

their kinds. Human life was a distinct and special creation. God created man, not from other animals, but directly from the dust of the earth. Each life form, whether animal or human, had its own genetic blueprint, with the ability to reproduce and perpetuate its own kind. The Bible does not teach that all living things in existence today have a common ancestry from 'simple' cellular organisms. It clearly insists on the special creation of different kinds of self-replicating life forms. In other words, from the beginning of life, fish have always been fish, birds have always been birds, and humans have always been humans. Paul informed the Corinthians: "All flesh is not the same flesh: but there is one kind of flesh of men, another flesh of beasts, another of fishes, and another of birds" (1 Cor 15:39).

We contend that there is a vital difference between micro-evolution, by which we mean variation within a species (which happens in real life), and macro-evolution, by which we mean transmutation of one species into another species (which does not happen in real life). Much of the textbook evidence being offered as proof of evolution is highly misleading in that it consists of examples of variation within a species being presented as if they were examples of macro-evolution. Two classic examples of this kind of misinformation are the famous peppered moths, and Darwin's finches. The reader should note that both before and after the observed changes in these case studies, the moths were still moths, and the finches were still finches! In fact, no example of macro-evolution has ever been observed.

Having made these observations, it is not our intention in this book to develop a critique of the theory of evolution. There are many helpful books on this subject readily available, and we refer the reader to the Bibliography at the back. What we wish to do now is to take another considered look at the subject of origins from the internal scriptural position. We shall look at what the Bible says about creation and origins. This, for the believer, is the final authority on the matter.

The Biblical Account of Origins

How refreshing it is to turn to the first verse in our Bible and to read that majestic opening statement:

"In the beginning God created the heaven and the earth" (Gen 1:1).

This is the beginning of truth, and is the foundation that underpins all revelation and knowledge. It is the key to understanding both earth history and universal history. The words evoke worship in the heart of every true believer, and yet it is a truth which any child can understand. The writer to the Hebrews informs us that such truth is apprehended by faith: "By faith we understand that the universe was created by the word of God, so that what is seen was not made out of things that are visible" (Heb 11:3 *ESV*).

It is striking to note how God invested His creation with value, meaning, function, and purpose. He endowed created things with value by describing them, no less than seven times, as *good*. We read that God saw that the light was *good*; earth and sea were *good*; grass, herbs and trees were *good*; the sun, moon and stars were *good*; whales, water life, and birds were *good*; beasts, cattle and creeping things were *good*; and finally, when God reviewed all that He had made, including man, it is said: "And God saw everything that he had made, and, behold, it was *very good*" (Gen 1:31).

Not only did God endow created things with value, He also gave them meaning and identity. This He did by applying the faculty of language and assigning names to them. We learn from the opening chapters of Genesis that God employs language and speech. He called the light *day*, and the darkness *night*; He called the firmament *heaven*; He called the dry land *earth*; and He called the gathered waters *sea*. The Psalmist tells us "He telleth the number of the stars; he calleth them all *by their names*" (Ps 147:4). Interestingly, God did not name the animals, but gave that privilege to Adam. God was going to share His love and fellowship with man. In fact, man would be entrusted with the care of His creation. We read in Genesis 2:19-20: "And out of the ground the LORD God formed every beast of the field, and every fowl of the air; and brought them unto Adam to see what he would call them: and whatsoever Adam called every living creature, that was the name thereof. And Adam gave names to all cattle, and to the fowl of the air, and to every beast of the field; but for Adam there was not found an help meet for him." It is humbling to note that the naming and classifying of animals is not an invention of our scientific age. The first person in history to assign names to animals and birds was Adam!

Not only do created things have value and meaning, they also have purpose and function. This becomes very evident on the fourth day of creation when God decorated the heavens with the sun, moon and stars. The purpose and function of the heavenly luminaries were to divide day from night, to be for signs, seasons, days and years, and to give light on the earth. The universe was designed as a functioning system. Further, we read concerning the sun, moon and stars, that God *set* them in the firmament of the heaven. In other words, the stars and planets are not in their present positions by chance, but by divine ordering.

I recall listening on BBC radio to the popular astronomer, Sir Patrick Moore, talking about the total solar eclipse of 1999. He drew attention to the fact that from the vantage point of earth, the sun and moon have exactly the same angular size. This means that during a solar eclipse, the moon's disc is seen by the observer on earth to be the same apparent size as that of the sun's disc. The moon therefore blocks out the sun's light so efficiently that the sun's corona becomes visible to the naked eye. Sir Patrick then added that as far as anyone knew, this phenomenon had come about purely by luck! Sir Patrick, to put it mildly, could hardly have been more wrong. We learn from Genesis that the ordering of heavenly bodies is not by luck, but by design. In fact, the properties of the universe and solar system are very finely tuned, within very narrow life-sustaining limits. The solar system was God's idea, and He arranged the sizes, orbits, and gravitational strengths of planets, moons, and sun. God set the earth's orbit at just the right distance from the sun, to facilitate the optimum heat, light, and gravitational effects necessary for life. It was God who made the stars, planets and moons and *set* them in the firmament.[20] But perhaps the greatest purpose of this vast creation was to display the glory and power of God. No one held the creation in greater awe than David, who began Psalm 19 with the words: "The heavens declare the glory of God; and the firmament sheweth his handywork" (Psalm 19:1). Further, David felt overwhelmed that the God of the heavens should be a *personal* God, intensely interested in mankind: "When I consider thy heavens, the work of thy fingers, the moon, and the stars, which thou hast ordained; what is man, that thou art mindful of him? And the son of man, that thou visitest him?" (Psalm 8:3-4).

Not only do the opening chapters of Genesis record the beginning of the physical universe, but they also give us the answer to that most baffling and elusive of questions, the origin of life. What is life, and how do we distinguish it from inanimate matter? The first organic life was created on the third day of the creation week. We read: "And God said, Let the earth bring forth grass, the herb yielding seed, and the fruit tree yielding fruit after his kind, whose seed is in itself, after his kind: and God saw that it was good" (Gen 1:11-12). Thus, living animals and plants etc. can be distinguished from inanimate matter by their ability to grow, develop, and reproduce. Notice that the fruit tree had *seed within itself, after its kind*. Thus self-replicating plant life was created on the third day.

Similarly, when God created sea life and birds on the fifth day, He did it *according to their kind*. The first mention, in the Bible, of God blessing anything is right here in connection with

---

[20] For an interesting study on the age of stars, see work by D. Russell Humphreys *Starlight and Time - Solving the Puzzle of Distant Starlight in a Young Universe* (Master Books, 2002). Humphreys rejects the current Big Bang theory which assumes an unbounded universe with no centre. He proposes that the universe is in fact bounded and has a centre. According to Einstein's theory of General Relativity, gravity distorts time. Therefore, in a bounded universe, and assuming the earth to be at the approximate centre, time will travel faster on earth than it will at the edge of the universe. This means that while six days are passing on earth, many millions of years will have passed at the edge of the universe. Without being dogmatic, Humphrey's cosmology makes a most interesting hypothesis, consistent with both the Genesis six-day account of creation, and Einstein's theory of General Relativity.

sea life and birds: "And God blessed them, saying, Be fruitful, and multiply, and fill the waters in the seas, and let fowl multiply in the earth" (Gen 1:22). The creatures were thus able to reproduce and multiply, not in a chaotic and non-directional way, but exactly as God had made them, *according to their kind*. The diversity of life in the sea is far higher than anyone could imagine. It is estimated that each millilitre of seawater contains one million bacteria and ten million viruses.

King David, who realised that the sea was teaming with life, expressed his fascination in poetry:

> O LORD, how manifold are thy works!
> In wisdom hast thou made them all:
> The earth is full of thy riches.
> So is this great and wide sea,
> Wherein are things creeping innumerable,
> Both small and great beasts.
> There go the ships:
> There is that leviathan,
> Whom Thou hast made to play therein.
> (Psalm 104:24-26)

It is good to note that David does not worship the creation, but cheerfully acknowledges the Creator. He ends his great creation psalm with the words:

> My meditation of him shall be sweet:
> I will be glad in the LORD.
> (Psalm 104:34).

One of the most delightful features of this creation is its great beauty. God, as the consummate Artist, made things to be gloriously beautiful. He could have made all things in utility grey, but in fact He made them in colour, with seemingly infinite variety in shape, form and texture. And to embellish His vast work of art, He added music! What pleasure we can have from the colour and texture of flowers, the taste and smell of food, the flight and music of birds. May we never lose that sense of wonder when we look at the exquisite engineering of a bird's feather, or the petal of a flower. God did not simply make a butterfly's wing to be functional, wonderful though that is, but He also made it a thing of beauty. We heartily concord and add our enthusiastic 'Amen' to the words of scripture at the close of the fifth day, "And God saw that it was good" (Gen 1:21).

Again, the same orderly principle of creation was in operation on the sixth day when God said "Let the earth bring forth the living creature *after his kind*, cattle, and creeping thing, and beast of the earth *after his kind*: and it was so" (Gen 1:24). However, God's crowning creation was yet to come. He was going to create an intelligent being with whom He could fellowship, and with whom He could share His love and goodness. Here then is the origin of man, the first human being, specially created on the sixth day: "And God said, Let us make man in our image, after our likeness: and let him have dominion over the fish of the sea, and over the fowl of the air, and over the cattle, and over all the earth, and over every creeping thing that creepeth on the earth. And God created man in his own image, in the image of God created he him; male and female created he them....And the LORD God formed man out of the dust of the ground, and breathed into his nostrils the breath of life; and man became a living soul" (Gen 1:26-27; 2:7).

The creation was completed on the sixth day, when God reviewed His own work, "And God saw every thing that he had made, and, behold, it was very good" (Gen 1:31). From the beginning, God wrote a spiritual dimension into the creation, in that He rested on the seventh day and *sanctified* it. This principle was later to be incorporated into the ten commandments from God to Israel: "Remember the Sabbath day to keep it holy....for in six days the LORD made heaven and earth, the sea, and all that in them is, and rested the seventh day: wherefore the LORD blessed the sabbath day, and hallowed it" (Ex 20:8-11). In other words, there was to be a regular time set apart for the enjoyment of the things of God. It was not to be a creature-centred, meaningless, dreary existence, but a meaningful relationship between God and His creatures. There was to be a holy inter-action between the Creator and the creation.

I stand in awe at the miracle of my own existence. Perhaps a greater miracle is the fact that I am able so to wonder! God created the conscious brain, with which I can conceptualise, rationalise, ponder and remember. The human mind is God's masterpiece. It was Pascal who said, "People can comprehend the stars, the stars comprehend nothing." God made us so that we might intelligently and lovingly fellowship and commune with Him. As well as giving us consciousness, God added that most awesome of gifts, the facility of language. In the Garden of Eden, the LORD God would come down and walk in the garden in the cool of the day (Gen 3:8). Thus the first man Adam, with his conscious and intelligent mind, was a special creation from the hand of God. It was man's privilege to serve God, to enjoy God, to fellowship with God, to worship God, and to love God. God made us *for Himself*, and to miss that truth is to miss the meaning of life.

The fellowship ended abruptly when Adam rebelled and sinned against God. The first man forfeited all the blessings of communion with God, and became a guilty, alienated, and helpless sinner. How could he be reconciled to the God whom he had offended? There was indeed salvation planned, although it would not be through Adam, but through the Lord from heaven. It would take the 'second man', the 'last Adam', to fulfil God's purposes in redemption, salvation, and reconciliation (1 Cor 15:45-47).

When we come to the New Testament, we are struck with the primary purpose of creation: "Thou art worthy, O Lord, to receive glory and honour and power: for thou hast created all things, and *for thy pleasure* they are and were created" (Rev 4:11). It pleased God to create the heaven and the earth, and to share them with His creatures. Indeed, creation is one of the great themes of worship in heaven.

Yet the New Testament informs us of another stupendous truth about the creation. God created all things 'through' or 'by' His Son. The Son of God was the agent in creation. John informs us, speaking of the Lord Jesus Christ: "All things were made by him; and without him was not anything made that was made" (John 1:3). Again speaking of Christ, Paul tells us: "For by him were all things created, that are in heaven, and that are in earth, visible and invisible, whether they be thrones, or dominions, or principalities, or powers: all things were created by him and for him: and he is before all things, and by him all things consist" (Col 1:16-17). The inspired writer to the Hebrews has something similar to say: "God...hath in these last days spoken unto us by his Son, whom he hath appointed heir of all things, by whom also he made the worlds; who being the brightness of his glory, and the express image of his person, and upholding all things by the word of his power, when he had by himself purged our sins, sat down on the right hand of the Majesty on high" (Heb 1:1-3).

We learn from these scriptures something about the past, the present, and the future of this creation. Concerning the past, it is said that the Son *created all things*. That is to say, the creation had a definite space-time beginning. Concerning the present, it is the Son who *sustains all things*, and by Him, *all things consist*. Concerning the future, God has appointed His Son to be the *Heir of all things*, the *Firstborn of all creation* (i.e. the inheritor of creation). The universe was made *by* Him and *for* Him.

How will this universe end? The writer to the Hebrews predicted, quoting from Psalm 102 and attributing the words as being addressed to the Son: "And, Thou, Lord, in the beginning hast laid the foundation of the earth; and the heavens are the works of thine hands: they shall perish; but thou remainest; and they shall all wax old as doth a garment; and as a vesture shalt thou fold them up, and they shall be changed: but thou art the same, and thy years shall not fail" (Heb 1:10-12). A discarded garment is a striking metaphor to describe the demise of heaven and earth. This creation will be folded up and changed, just as a person would discard an old item of clothing.

Peter refers to the judgement which will come on the

universe: "But the day of the Lord will come like a thief in the night; in the which the heavens shall pass away with a great noise, and the elements shall melt with fervent heat, the earth also and the works that are therein shall be burned up....Nevertheless we, according to his promise, look for new heavens and a new earth, wherein dwelleth righteousness" (2 Pet 3:10-13). John also looks forward to the day when the holy city, new Jerusalem, will come down from God out of heaven, prepared as a bride adorned for her husband. That will take place at the inauguration of the new creation: "And I saw a new heaven and a new earth: for the first heaven and the first earth were passed away; and there was no more sea" (Rev 21:1-2). It is far outside the remit of science to predict such a thing as a divine judgement on the universe, and the bringing in of a new heaven and a new earth. Such things are only made known by revelation, and are understood by faith. The Lord Jesus said that heaven and earth would pass away, but His words would never pass away. No part of scripture will ever need to be deleted, updated, or revised. Further, the church shall be with Christ forever. C.S.Lewis put it nicely: "The Church will outlive the universe; in it the individual person will outlive the universe. Everything that is joined to the immortal head will share his immortality."[21]

Before leaving the grand subject of creation, we must ask ourselves an important question concerning the issue of interpretation. Are the opening chapters of Genesis to be understood as history or allegory? Do they give a factual account of real people and events, or are they some kind of non-literal, legendary tales that ought to be interpreted symbolically? We shall look to the internal evidence of the Bible and offer three reasons why the opening chapters of Genesis must be considered as factual and not mythical.

First, the Bible contains numerous genealogies all of which branch from a common ancestor, Adam. The book of Genesis

---

[21] Lewis, C.S. "Membership" in *Fern-seed and Elephants* (Fount Paperbacks, 1978) p.21.

establishes that Adam and Eve were the parents of Cain and Abel (Gen 4:1-2), and that Eve was "the mother of all living" (Gen 3:20). We are given the genealogy of Cain's descendants in Gen 4:17-24. Abel had no descendants, having been murdered by his brother Cain. It was Seth who took Abel's place, and his genealogy is given in Gen 5, from Adam through to Noah's three sons: Shem, Ham, and Japheth. The world was repopulated from these three brothers after the flood, and their respective descendants are listed in Gen 10. In Gen 11 another genealogy is given, this time confined to the line of Shem through his son Arphaxad, and continuing to the patriarch Abraham. In Genesis 25, we read about the descendants of Abraham, through his sons Ishmael and Isaac. The line of Isaac, Jacob and the twelve patriarchs is continued in Gen 35. The traceable link from Adam to Judah, through Abraham, Isaac and Jacob, is of the utmost importance to the unfolding drama of salvation. The book of Genesis is not written in the language of legend or symbol, but rather in the careful and accurate language of recorded history.

Another Old Testament book containing genealogies is 1 Chronicles, where the first chapter begins with the words: "Adam, Sheth, Enosh" (1 Chron 1:1). Numerous side branches are given as the book progresses, but the focus keeps returning to the line of Adam, Seth, Noah, Shem, Abraham, Judah, and hence to David. Three names begin to emerge as the vital links in the genealogical tree: Adam, Abraham, David.

The towering importance of these three historical persons becomes evident when we turn to the New Testament. Matthew begins his gospel with the words: "The book of the generation of Jesus Christ, the son of David, the son of Abraham" (Mat 1:1). The tree of descent given in the first chapter of Matthew establishes the Lord's right to the throne of David through Joseph, who was His legal, though not natural, father. When we come to Luke's record, the genealogy of the Lord Jesus is traced through David and Abraham, back to Adam: "Which was the son of Enos, which was the son of Seth, which was the son of Adam, which was the son of God" (Luke 3:23-38). Here the royal descent of the Lord Jesus is established (on Mary's side) through David and Nathan (not Solomon), right back to Adam. It is evident that Luke regarded the opening chapters of Genesis as describing real people. The New Testament genealogies fully confirm the historicity of Genesis.

The second reason for considering the book of Genesis as literal history is the manner in which the Lord Jesus made reference to its people and events. For example, when the Lord was asked a question about marriage and divorce, He responded by pointing out that the institution of marriage pre-dated the law of Moses and went back to creation. The Lord clearly alluded to Genesis 1:27 when He said, "But from the beginning of the creation God made them male and female" (Mk 10:6). Again, when speaking of the great tribulation which will come on the earth in a future day, the Lord Jesus said: "For in those days shall be affliction, such as was not from the beginning of the creation which God created unto this time, neither shall be" (Mk 13:19). Further, the Lord certainly held Abel to be a historical person, seeing that He held His own generation to be morally responsible for his murder: "That upon you may come all the righteous blood shed upon the earth, from the blood of righteous Abel unto the blood of Zacharias son of Barachias, whom ye slew between the temple and the altar" (Mt 23:35). It would be a very strange thing to be held accountable for an allegorical murder! Finally, the Lord's references to Noah's flood, and to the later destruction of Sodom, clearly establish the historicity of Genesis.

The third reason is that the doctrinal writings of the New Testament presuppose and demand a literal-historical understanding of Genesis.
Paul informs us that sin, death, offence, judgment, condemnation, and disobedience entered into the world by one man, Adam. Equally, the blessings of grace, justification, righteousness, obedience and eternal life came by one man, Jesus Christ. We quote the following extended passage to

highlight the importance of understanding Adam to be the literal ancestor of us all:

"Wherefore, as by *one man* sin entered into the world, and death by sin; and so death passed upon all men, for that all have sinned: (For until the law sin was in the world: but sin is not imputed when there is no law. Nevertheless death reigned from *Adam* to Moses, even over them that had not sinned after the similitude of *Adam's* transgression, who is the figure of him that was to come. But not as the offence, so also is the free gift. For if through *the offence of one* many be dead, much more the grace of God, and the gift by grace, which is *by one man, Jesus Christ*, hath abounded unto many. And not as it was *by one that sinned*, so is the gift: for the judgment was *by one to condemnation*, but the free gift is of many offences unto justification. For if *by one man's offence* death reigned *by one*; much more they which receive abundance of grace and of the gift of righteousness shall reign in life *by one, Jesus Christ*.) Therefore as *by the offence of one* judgment came upon all men to condemnation; even so by *the righteousness of one* the free gift came upon all men unto justification of life. For as *by one man's disobedience* many were made sinners, so *by the obedience of one* shall many be made righteous. Moreover the law entered, that the offence might abound. But where sin abounded, grace did much more abound: that as sin hath reigned unto death, even so might grace reign through righteousness unto eternal life by Jesus Christ our Lord. (Romans 5:12-21)

This passage teaches us that because of Adam's sin, we have all been born 'damaged goods' so to speak. But happily there is salvation through another, Jesus Christ. Adam was the "figure of him that was to come" in the sense that he was the federal head of the human race, just as the Lord Jesus Christ was to become the federal head of the new creation. Each and every person is either 'in Adam' (i.e. in his or her sins) or 'in Christ' (i.e. saved).

This doctrine is developed further by Paul in his first letter to the Corinthians. On the subject of death and resurrection,

Paul has this to say: "For since by man came death, by man came also the resurrection from the dead. For as in Adam all die, even so in Christ shall all be made alive" (1 Cor 15:21-22). Again we can see that God views every person as either 'in Adam', or 'in Christ'.

The thought is developed yet further by Paul, as he contrasts Adam and Christ: "And so it is written, The first man Adam was made a living soul; the last Adam was made a quickening (life-giving) spirit. Howbeit that was not first which is spiritual, but that which is natural; and afterward that which is spiritual. The first man is of the earth, earthy: the second man is the Lord from heaven" (1 Cor 15:45-47). The Lord Jesus is described as the "last Adam" because there will never be another head of the race. He is described as the "second man" because He has introduced a new order of humanity. There are only two men in history who matter as far as our standing before God is concerned: the first man, Adam; and the second man, Christ. We are either in Adam or in Christ. There is no third option. We are linked to Adam by natural birth; we can only be linked to Christ by *new* birth. In other words, we must be born again (see John 3:3ff).

It can be seen from Paul's doctrine of salvation that Adam was a real historical person, and that his fall in Genesis 3 was a catastrophic space-time event which brought ruin to us all. But there are yet further doctrines which are based on the historicity of Genesis. For example, it is a principle of New Testament church practice that women are to learn in silence, and are not allowed to have authority over men. The reason for this prohibition is not cultural, in spite of what today's feminists might say, but rather has to do with the sequence of certain events as recorded in Genesis: "For Adam was first formed, then Eve. And Adam was not deceived, but the woman being deceived was in the transgression" (1 Tim 2:13-14). The headship of the man over the woman, in this passage as well as in 1 Cor 11, is based on the creatorial order of Genesis.

Paul also appeals to the case of Eve to warn the Corinthians of the possibility of their being misled by a false gospel: "But I fear, lest by any means, as the serpent beguiled Eve through his subtilty, so your minds should be corrupted from the simplicity that is in Christ" (2 Cor 11:3). Once again, the historicity of Genesis is assumed by Paul.

We submit that the doctrines of salvation and headship, as developed by Paul, presuppose and demand a literal-historical view of the whole book of Genesis. It is not simply that the second half of Genesis, from Abraham on, is historical, while the first eleven chapters are mythical. We hold and insist that the first eleven chapters are also historically true. Francis Schaeffer made the point well: "...our thesis is that the Bible, including the first eleven chapters of Genesis, sets forth propositional truth, both where it touches history and the cosmos and where it touches religious matters. Because almost everyone accepts that the second half of Genesis, namely, from Abraham on, is historic, it is important to consider the indications that the whole book of Genesis is a unit."[22]

We conclude that the Biblical genealogies, together with the words of the Lord Jesus as recorded in the four Gospels, and the doctrinal teaching of the New Testament, all affirm the historicity of the book of Genesis. Men of every generation can have total confidence in the reliability and truth of the Bible. Further, we totally reject the idea that the universe is a meaningless cosmic accident, or that man is the result of blind evolutionary processes. It is the Lord who is the Maker of heaven and earth. We fully concord with the Psalmist when he affirms God's title deeds to this creation, "The heavens are thine, the earth also is thine: as for the world and the fulness thereof, thou hast founded them" (Psalm 89:11).

---

[22] Schaeffer, Francis A. *No Final Conflict* (Hodder and Stoughton, 1975) p.18.

CHAPTER 6

The Gospel and the 'Postmodern' World

It was the Enlightenment philosopher Diderot who said, "I love that philosophy which raises up humanity." This optimistic view of human nature was the leading premise of Enlightenment humanism. In the progress model of the Enlightenment, God had been pushed out of the centre and had been replaced by human reason. Immanuel Kant, regarded as the high priest of Enlightenment humanism, claimed to be a believer in God. However, Kant's God was nothing more than a postulate of human reason. Kant did not believe in the personal transcendent God of the Bible, but in a God who was merely a kind of secondary hypothesis. Nevertheless, it was a belief in a God of sorts. But the idea of such a minimal God would prove temporary, and impossible to sustain.

A new kind of humanism began to emerge in the twentieth century. Abandoning the notions of the deist God that had come from Enlightenment thought, many humanists began to openly profess atheism. Thus developed the movement generally known as 'secular humanism'. As the twentieth century progressed, scientists, philosophers, and theologians increasingly based their work and methodologies on humanistic assumptions. As a result, society became thoroughly secular in its outlook, especially in the areas of ethics and morality.

It is interesting to note that all humanists taught ethics. Morality was held to be necessary by both kinds of humanists, whether of the classic Enlightenment variety (such as Immanuel Kant), or of the later secular atheistic kind (such as Isaac Asimov). Norman Geisler, describing the Humanist Manifesto

II (1973) as a "strong, urgent, moral, and religious call", goes on to evaluate secular humanism as, "atheistic, naturalistic, evolutionistic, socialistic, relativistic, and still optimistic that humankind can save itself."[23] However, not all modern thinkers were comfortable with the progress model of humanism. For example, does a humanist have any right to speak about morality? If a humanist teaches that there is no God, and that men can decide their own rules of morality, how can he know if he is right or wrong in his decision? Again, do the terms 'right or wrong' have any real objective meaning? If there is no God, then logically there cannot be any moral absolutes. Moreover, if there are no moral absolutes, our own ideas of right or wrong are purely relative, and cannot be applied universally. The secular humanist insists that God does not exist, and that men are capable of deciding what is correct moral behaviour. But if there is no God, then there is no base for morality. It was G.K.Chesterton who incisively observed, "Humanists live off the moral capital of Christianity." Not all humanists were happy with this paradox.

Arguably, the most notorious philosopher who ever lived was Friedrich Nietzsche (1844-1900). The starting point of philosophy for Nietzsche was the non-existence of God, from which he argued that man was alone and must fend for himself. According to the Christian writer Colin Brown, Nietzsche "had nothing but scorn for those who denied the Christian idea of God but sought to salvage Christian morality. For Nietzsche there must be a clean sweep. Man must start from scratch, deciding what is right and wrong by his own will."[24] Nietzsche held that truth is merely a cultural necessity, an expedient condition of language. Nietzsche's influence upon European literature and philosophy is said to have been incalculable. Not only is Nietzsche reckoned to have been the philosophical inspiration for Hitler's *Mein Kampf*, but he is also known as the founding father of postmodernism. We can reliably judge the

---

[23] Geisler, Norman L. *Baker Encyclopedia of Christian Apologetics* (Baker Books, Grand Rapids, 2000) p.340.
[24] C Brown *Philosophy and the Christian Faith* (Inter-varsity Press, London, reprint 1974) p.140.

character and worth of a movement by tracing it to its source. The Lord Jesus said "Either make the tree good, and his fruit good, or else make the tree corrupt, and his fruit corrupt: for the tree is known by its fruit" (Mat 12:33). Nietzsche, who lived his life ranting against God and Christianity, died alone and insane at fifty six years of age.

Many thinkers in France in the 1970s, inspired by the writings of Nietzsche, faced up to the implications of their atheistic beliefs and abandoned the humanists' pretensions to progress, truth and morality. Attempting to remain consistent with their atheistic presuppositions, and foolishly going where their beliefs would take them, they entered a cul-de-sac of waylessness, lostness and nihilism. Truth became relative, ethics became situational, and life became meaningless. Thus began the movement known as *postmodernism*.

The Postmodern Era

The postmodern outlook has impacted on all the academic disciplines such as philosophy, theology, architecture, political studies, psychology, sociology, media studies, literary theory, geography, history, economics, jurisprudence, anthropology, and even commercial marketing.[25] How should we preach the gospel to someone with a postmodern mindset? That is the question that we shall presently address, but first we shall outline some of the features of postmodernity.

What is the difference between modernism and postmodernism? The following will serve as a very simple and short answer to this question:

The leading premise of modernism is that man can discover truth by unaided human reason, whereas the leading premise of postmodernism is that there is no such thing as truth to be discovered.

When did modernity end and postmodernity begin? The era of modernity has been conveniently placed within a period of approximately 200 years. In 1789, the people of Paris stormed

---

[25] I was first introduced to postmodernism in the mid-1990s by my Professor of Retail Marketing, Stephen Brown, author of *Postmodern Marketing* (Routledge, London and New York, 1995).

the Bastille, marking the end of an old social order and the beginning of the modern age. In 1989, the people of Germany tore down the Berlin wall, and by doing so signalled the end of the modern age. Thus, the era of modernity began with the French Revolution and ended with the collapse of Communism. The Christian author Thomas Oden has written: "By *postmodern* we mean the course of actual history following the death of modernity. By *modernity* we mean the period, the ideology, and the malaise of the time from 1789 to 1989, from the Bastille to the Berlin Wall."[26]

Modernism was predicated on the idea of human reason, championing the concepts of rational science, universal laws, absolute truths, objective knowledge, and above all, progress. Postmodernism, on the other hand, rejects these old certainties as untenable, and has put in their place the ideas of relativism, contextualism and pluralism. The postmodern agenda is to deconstruct the progress model of modernity. In short, we are talking about two very different approaches to the nature of knowledge. The French philosopher Jean-FranÁois Lyotard (1924-1998) has described postmodernism as the "gradual decline of the old ideologies and belief systems of the modern world".[27] Lyotard spoke of the 'demise of metanarratives', by which he meant the collapse of the universal truths and assumptions that underpin western civilisation. He dismissed the modernist idea of progress as a myth.

At this point we would make the observation, from a Christian point of view, that postmodernism is right in so far as it exposes the false foundations of modernism. In fact, postmodernism can rightly be regarded as a corrective to humanism, and as modernism's declaration of bankruptcy. But we also contend that postmodernism is not so much a reaction or departure from modernism, but is the *logical conclusion* of its non-Christian presuppositions. Postmodernism is anti-

[26] Oden, Thomas "The Death of Modernity and Postmodern Evangelical Spirituality" in *The Challenge of Postmodernism* Ed. David S. Dockery (BridgePoint Books, USA, 1995) p.20.
[27] Oliver, Martin *History of Philosophy* (Hamlyn, GB, 1997) p.171.

129

foundational, having demolished the foundations of modernism and replaced them with nothing. This is what Lyotard describes as the 'postmodern condition'.

The university student who is required to research this subject will be introduced to the works of philosophers such as Michael Foucalt, Jean Baudrillard, Jacques Derrida, Richard Rorty and Jean-François Lyotard. However, the purpose of this book is not to serve as a philosophy textbook, but rather to examine what the Bible says about such ideas, especially in relation to the doctrine of the gospel. With this in mind, we shall now consider some of the leading themes of postmodernism in light of the revealed truth of scripture.

Relativism
Relativism is not a new idea. The Greek philosopher, Protagoras (c.480-411 BC), believed that nothing was exclusively true or false, but that what is true for one person may be false for another. In his famous dictum "man is the measure of all things", Protagoras was stating that there is no general or objective truth. This leads to the unavoidable conclusion that stealing or adultery can be both good and bad, i.e. good for one person and bad for another. This is the mind-set of today's postmodernist. According to this view, it is not possible to make a definitive statement that something like Hindu widow-immolation is wrong in any absolute sense. The ideas of right and wrong are socially determined; therefore widow burning may be wrong for one culture, while it is right for another. The same could be said about cannibalism. It is, in the end, a relative judgement, not a moral absolute.

What is truth? A dictionary might define 'true' as agreeing with fact or reality, not false or wrong. In other words, truth is that which corresponds with reality or reflects reality - what really is.[28] A belief can be said to be true when it accurately reflects and corresponds with the fact. Given this 'correspondence' understanding of truth, there is clearly such

---

[28] Josh McDowell *The New Evidence that Demands a Verdict* (Nelson, 1999) pp.585-6.

a thing as objective or absolute truth. The relativist, however, rejects the idea of objective truth and replaces it with the notion of subjective truth, that is to say - truth or reality is determined by the subject. It is at this point that we can see that the basic postmodernist premise is self-defeating. The postmodernist states that there is no such thing as absolute truth. But if that statement is true, then what is being said cannot be true in any absolute sense. To state in absolute terms that there is no such thing as absolute truth is self-referentially inconsistent. In short, it is nonsense.

According to the *Internet Encyclopedia of Philosophy*,[29] there are many different kinds of relativism which all have two features in common.

1) They all assert that one thing (e.g. moral values, beauty, knowledge, taste, or meaning) is relative to some particular framework or standpoint (e.g. the individual subject, a culture, an era, a language, or a conceptual scheme).

2) They all deny that any standpoint is uniquely privileged over all others.

These leading premises of relativism inevitably result in the idea that a propositional statement can be both true and false at the same time. That is to say, it is a case of 'both/and'. However, rational and sane people have been used to thinking in terms of 'either/or' rather than 'both/and'. A statement is *either* true *or* it is false, rather than *both* true *and* false.

Let us consider an example from the Bible. The Lord Jesus, when He had been asked by the chief priests and elders to explain His authority for doing the things that He did, responded with a counter-question. It is most instructive to observe the form of the question. The Lord replied, "I also will ask you one thing, which if ye tell me, I in like wise will tell you by what authority I do these things. The baptism of John, whence was it? from heaven or of men?" (Matt 21:24-25). It is vital to note that the question was being asked in an 'either/or' framework. Either John's baptism was from heaven *or* it was

---

[29] Westacott, Emrys "Relativism" in *The Internet Encyclopedia of Philosophy* [http://www.iep.utm.edu/r/relativi.htm] (December 04, 2004).

of men. The Lord was allowing no other option. The postmodern answer to the question would have been that John's baptism was *both* from heaven, *and* of men, depending on the person's subjective and cultural framework. That view is untenable, if not absurd. If John's baptism was from heaven, then it was not of men, regardless of culture and context. The statement is true or false in the objective sense, regardless of whether a person believes it or not. Thus propositional truth is presented in scripture as an 'either/or' reality, never as a 'both/and' possibility. The postmodern view of the nature of truth is unscriptural in the extreme.

Not only is postmodernism unscriptural, but it is also philosophically unsound. The most elementary law of logic states: *A cannot be non-A.* When a postmodernist states that something can be *both* true *and* untrue at the same time, he is violating this basic Non-Contradiction Principle. In other words, the postmodernist's approach to propositional truth is incoherent and self-contradictory.

We shall take another example from the Bible, this time from the writings of Paul. Is the resurrection true? It is no exaggeration to say that the claims of Christianity stand or fall on the historic event of the resurrection of Christ. If Christ rose bodily from the dead, then the claims of scripture are fully validated. If Christ did not rise bodily from the dead then the claims of scripture are rendered invalid. There is no third possibility, and Paul presents the options in terms of an 'either/or' reality. Either Christ rose or He did not. Paul states, "If Christ be not raised, your faith is vain" (1 Cor 15:17). Happily, Paul is able to counter this hypothetical notion by the assertion: "But now is Christ risen from the dead, and become the firstfruits of them that slept" (1 Cor 15:20). When we ask if the resurrection is true, we are asking in terms of an 'either/or' framework. On the other hand, a postmodernist would answer the question in a 'both/and' framework. He would claim that it is equally true to say that Christ *both* rose *and* never rose from the dead. We can see that something terrible has happened to the concept of truth. For the postmodernist, it does not matter whether Christ *actually* rose from the dead or not, but it is simply a matter of a person's cultural and contextual response. It is therefore no exaggeration to say that the postmodern approach to truth is self-contradictory nonsense.

The claim of postmodernism is that all meaning, truth, and value are man-made. What happens when this logic is applied to the most fundamental of all questions - Does God exist? Again, the question demands to be answered in an 'either/or' framework. Either God exists or He does not. The postmodern answer takes us into the regions of the absurd. The postmodern writer Don Cupitt is representative of the new approach when he advocates a non-realist, rather than a realist, interpretation of religion. Having quoted Jung, Schweitzer and Wittgenstein as non-realists, Cupitt urges his readers "not to ask the plain man's political-realist question, 'Does this man think that God exists or not?', a question that narrows and deforms the issues, but instead to set aside 'existence' in favour of 'meaning' and ask the much more illuminating question, 'What job does God do, what part does he play, to what use is the idea of God put in this man's thought?' From the new non-realist viewpoint a person believes in God if the idea of God does some real work and plays a constitutive part in his thinking and in shaping his way of life."[30] This is nothing less than educated idolatry. It is telling people to make their own god, and to fashion him according to their own particular preferences. Cupitt has attempted to deconstruct Christianity and replace it with his own postmodern Christian-Buddhist-Humanist scheme.

What is the truth about God? Can we speak in the objective and realist sense of a *'true* God' who made heaven and earth, or can we only speak in the subjective sense of a god of our own making? God made Himself known to Israel in the first two commandments: "I am the LORD thy God, which have brought thee out of the land of Egypt, out of the house of bondage. Thou shalt have no other gods before me. Thou shalt not make unto thee any graven image, or any likeness of any

---

[30] Cupitt, Don *The Sea of Faith* (BBC, UK, 1984) p.245.

thing that is in heaven above, or that is in the earth beneath, or that is in the water under the earth: Thou shalt not bow thyself to them, nor serve them: for I the LORD thy God am a jealous God, visiting the iniquity of the fathers upon the children unto the third and fourth generation of them that hate me; and shewing mercy unto thousands of them that love me, and keep my commandments" (Ex 20:3-6). This teaches that God is personal and that He acts in the best interests of His people, interacting with them on moral grounds. The people of Israel were to be in a living, loving and exclusive fellowship with God.

If we were to ask Jeremiah if he believed in God in the objective and realist sense, we should receive his reply; "But the LORD is the *true* God, and an everlasting king: at his wrath the earth shall tremble, and the nations shall not be able to abide his indignation. Thus shall ye say unto them, The gods that have not made the heavens and the earth, even they shall perish from the earth, and from under these heavens. He hath made the earth by his power, he hath established the world by his wisdom, and hath stretched out the heavens by his discretion" (Jer 10:10-12).

Should we put the same question to Paul, he would remind us of his words to the Thessalonian believers, how they "had turned to God from idols to serve the *living and true* God" (1 Thes 1:9). Similarly, John would point us to the concluding remarks of his first letter: "And we know that the Son of God is come, and hath given us an understanding, that we may know him that is *true*, and we are in him that is *true*, even in his Son Jesus Christ. This is the *true* God, and eternal life" (1 John 5:20).

Many more scriptures could be quoted to prove that God exists in the real and objective sense. We quote the words of the Lord Jesus to His Father on the night of His betrayal: "And this is life eternal, that they might know thee the only *true* God, and Jesus Christ, whom thou hast sent" (John 17:3).

There is indeed such a thing as truth in the absolute, universal, and eternal sense. Further, it is God's desire that all men should come to know the truth. Paul informs us that God our Saviour "will have all men to be saved, and to come unto the knowledge of the *truth*" (1 Tim 2:4). The Lord Jesus claimed: "I am the way, the *truth*, and the life: no man cometh unto the Father but by me" (John 14:6). The Lord Himself is the whole truth about God; He is the "brightness of his glory, and the express image of his person" (Heb 1:3). He is "the image of the invisible God" (Col 1:15). John tells us that "In the beginning was the Word, and the Word was with God, and the Word was God....And the Word was made flesh, and dwelt among us, (and we beheld his glory as of the only begotten of the Father,) full of grace and *truth*" (John 1:1,14).

The key thought behind relativism is that 'truth' is always contextually interpreted within a particular frame-work or standpoint, especially that of language. Indeed, a characteristic feature of postmodern philosophy is its preoccupation with language. Gene Veith has written: "Postmodernists base this new relativism and the view that all meaning is socially constructed on a particular view of language. This set of theories, along with the analytical method that they make possible, can be referred to as 'deconstructionism'. Postmodernist theories begin with the assumption that language cannot render truths about the world in an objective way. Language by its very nature, shapes what we think. Since language is a cultural creation, meaning is ultimately a social construction."[31] In other words, we are being asked to believe that language does not reveal meaning, rather, language constructs meaning.

The philosopher Ludwig Wittgenstein (1889-1951), whose ideas about language have been enthusiastically adopted by the postmoderns, insisted that reality does not determine language, rather language determines reality. There is no transcendent God out there, only silence. There is language and there is the human realm, and nothing else. In the end, there are only facts about language, and we, through language, constitute our world. What are we to make of all this? Perhaps

---

[31] Veith, Gene Edward *Guide to Contemporary Culture* (Crossway Books, Leicester, 1994) p.51.

the first word that comes to mind is nonsense! That would be entirely appropriate, and would have been approved by the early Wittgenstein himself, who had described his own writings as nonsensical and meaningless. He believed that he had brought about the end of philosophy, and his destructive approach had even his Cambridge colleague, the famous Bertrand Russell, uncertain about his own work.

This approach to language and its meaning is taken yet further by the postmodern philosopher Jacques Derrida (1930-2004). Derrida advocated a post-structuralist approach to literary texts, by which he meant that language has no objectively identifiable meaning, and that therefore texts allow any number of interpretations. Derrida's method is to deconstruct the text to reveal many layers of meaning, but without allowing any single fixed meaning. It is no longer permissible, according to Derrida, to analyse a piece of text by asking what the writer had meant when he wrote it. Instead, we can only ask - What does the text mean to me? In other words, there is no such thing as authorial intention! The book consists of *our reading* of the text. We decide the meaning. Interpretation of a text is therefore not finding out what meaning the writer intended, but is purely a subjective evaluation of multi-dimensional meanings. Meaning is never fixed, but is deferred indefinitely. For Derrida, there is no such thing as meaning - it always eludes us. The classic view of meaning has been deconstructed and replaced with non-meaning. This is clearly absurd. Alarmingly, Derrida is very influential in English literature departments to-day.

Again, we can see the self-defeating nature of postmodernist thought. What happens when we apply Derrida's own rule to his own writings? According to Derrida, we must not ask what an author meant, but rather we must interpret the text subjectively. So presumably that includes the writings of Derrida himself. Therefore, it does not matter what Derrida meant, it only matters how I interpret the text. You and I can put two entirely different interpretations on what Derrida said, and neither of us will be wrong. We need not take seriously anything that Derrida has written, since by his own rule we must not ask what he meant when he wrote it!

The American writer Richard Rorty (1931-) is one of the most widely read philosophers alive today. Rorty argues that there is no such thing as certain knowledge or objective truth. There is simply no truth out there. Consequently, modern philosophy with its quest for truth, has reached a dead end. For Rorty, truth is no more than a condition of language. Just as a text allows for multiple readings, so does the world. Rorty claims that what is true is nothing more than what we agree to be true. This in turn is more a matter of social and historical context rather than scientific or objective enquiry. Rorty is not interested in whether something is true or false, as long as it coheres with our system of beliefs. Coherence, not truth, is the criterion by which we judge our beliefs. Rorty applies this approach not only to ethics and morality, but also to the natural sciences.

Why mention Wittgenstein, Derrida, Rorty and this meaningless nonsense? I merely want to point out that when people begin a mental journey with non-Christian presuppositions, the road will lead them into increasing waylessness. When men declare that there is no God out there, and try to shape their own world on that presupposition, they will in the end arrive at the inevitable conclusion that all is meaningless. History is strewn with examples of brilliant minds who have travelled this route and have sought to take others with them. The philosophy of Nietzsche led to nihilism, and became the rationale for Nazism and postmodernism; the philosophy of Sartre and the Existentialists led to despair and suicide; while the philosophy of Marx led to human slavery. The postmodern journey has led to a barren and frightening landscape of irrationalism, meaninglessness and absurdity. Postmodern man is lost, and has forgotten where he came from.

Should this surprise us? The first person in history to foresee postmodernism was none other than King Solomon. On reflecting what life is like if our only reference point is "under the sun" (i.e. leaving God out) , Solomon observed:

"Vanity of vanities, saith the Preacher, vanity of vanities; all is vanity." (Eccl 1:2)

The postmodern condition has been well described by Solomon in the book of Ecclesiastes. Solomon had studied various human pursuits such as wisdom, pleasure, folly, toil, advancement, and riches. He had concluded that, without God, all such human activities are ultimately vain, empty, and meaningless. As always, the Bible is up to date.

For the Christian, life is not meaningless, but rather it is a holy and purposive fellowship with the living and true God. Our lives, by God's grace, are eternally significant. We can trace all our blessings back to the centre cross at Calvary, and to "the Son of God who loved me, and gave himself for me" (Gal 2:20). Meaning! What greater meaning could there ever be?

Before leaving the subject of relativism we shall observe one more thing about language as used in scripture. On the subject of God's language, Veith writes: "The universe was created by a series of speech acts. The order of the universe, the reality of scientific laws, the language-like codes of DNA, and the mathematical consistency of physics all have their origin in the Word of God."[32] In the Bible, God speaks to men in their own language, in verbalised propositional form. We hasten to add that He speaks about truth, not in a socially constructed or relative sense, but in the real, absolute, universal and eternal sense. We happily concord with Paul's beautiful doxology: "To God only wise, be glory through Jesus Christ for ever. Amen" (Rom 16:27).

Pluralism

We now live, so we are told, in a multi-faith, pluralistic, world. Stated simply, pluralism is the idea that no single religion is uniquely privileged over all other religions. Hence we hear people speak of learning from the richness and diversity of other faiths. Jesus Christ is relegated as one guru among many gurus. I do not know who writes the speeches for the Queen, but in

---

[32] Ibid. p.65.

her 2001 Christmas message, she offered this unfortunate piece of postmodern thought:

"Whether we believe in God or not, I think most of us have a sense of the spiritual, that recognition of a deeper meaning and purpose in our lives, and I believe that this sense flourishes despite the pressures of our world. This spirituality can be seen in the teachings of other great faiths. Of course religion can be divisive, but the Bible, the Koran, and the sacred texts of the Jews and Hindus, Buddhists and Sikhs, are all sources of divine inspiration and practical guidance passed down through the generations."

The sentiments expressed in this broadcast were 'politically correct', and deceptively appealing. How should Christians respond to this type of thinking? Is it true that there is not just one truth, but many truths; not just one way, but many ways? Are all religions simply different aspects of the same totality? Again, we are indebted to Veith for a helpful insight into the theme of pluralism: "Postmodernism stresses tolerance, pluralism, and multiculturalism, but in its dismissal of all beliefs, it trivializes all cultures and tolerates none."[33]

When Thomas spoke for the disciples and asked the Lord Jesus how they might know the way, the Lord replied with an absolute and exclusive truth-claim: "Jesus saith unto him, I am the way, the truth, and the life: no man cometh unto the Father but by me" (John 14:6). Similarly, when Peter was answering the high priest regarding Jesus of Nazareth, he said, "Neither is there salvation in any other: for there is none other name under heaven given among men, whereby we must be saved" (Acts 4:12).

Clearly, the Bible presents Christ and His saving work as being unique, exclusive, absolute and eternal. This does not sit easily, to say the least, with modern ideas about pluralism. Comparative religion invites us to compare the great faiths and to observe what they have in common.

Let us do exactly that for a moment - let us compare the

---

[33] Ibid. p.72.

Person of Christ with the religious leaders of the world. Can any of the following observations be made about any other man who ever lived?

The Prophecies concerning Him

What other man had prophecies spoken and written about him for hundreds of years before his birth? The Lord Jesus was spoken of in the Law, the Psalms and the Prophets. His birth, life, miracles, suffering, death, burial, resurrection and ascension were all foretold in accurate and exact details. This could be said of no other man.

The manner of His birth

It is recorded that Joseph knew not Mary until "she had brought forth her firstborn son" (Mat 1:25). The Lord Jesus was born of a virgin, as foretold by the prophet Isaiah: "Therefore the LORD himself shall give you a sign; Behold, a virgin shall conceive, and bear a son, and shall call his name Immanuel" (Isaiah 7:14). The birth of the Lord Jesus is unique in the whole of human history.

The manner of His life

The earthly ministry of Christ consisted of teaching, preaching and healing. He taught with unrivalled wisdom and insight. His preaching was with authority and power. He spoke of life and death, value and meaning, time and eternity. He proclaimed Himself to be the Bread of God that had come down from heaven, and who gives life to the world. His miracles demonstrated that He had power over disease, death, nature, and the spirit world. The scriptures say of Him that He "did no sin" (1 Pet 2:22). His life was absolutely holy and righteous. Every other leader of men, whether from the East or the West, has possessed a sinful nature. It was the Lord Jesus Christ alone who possessed holy, sinless, humanity. If one were to search all history for an ideal and exemplary life, the search would lead supremely to Jesus Christ.

The meaning of His death

Did any man ever die for me in the sense of voluntarily becoming answerable for my sins? Paul tells us, "Christ died for our sins according to the scriptures" (1 Cor 15:3). Peter informs us that "Christ also hath once suffered for sins, the just for the unjust, that he might bring us to God, being put to death in the flesh..." (1 Pet 3:18). The writer to the Hebrews tells us that the Lord Jesus was made a little lower than angels "that he by the grace of God should taste death for every man" (Heb 2:9). His death was an atoning death in that it made satisfaction for sin. The Lord Jesus has "put away sin by the sacrifice of himself" (Heb 9:26). Returning to the question - can you find me another Saviour who died for my sins that I might be saved from their penalty and power? Has any one else died for me, to bring me to God? Such things could not be said of any man, except our Lord Jesus Christ. We must conclude that the death of the Lord Jesus has unique meaning and saving power. His death was a sacrifice in the stead of others. He died as our sin-bearer; He died for our sins. No one else died for me in that sense. It was Christ alone who "when he had by himself purged our sins, sat down on the right hand of the Majesty on high" (Heb 1:3).

The fact of His resurrection

Who among the leaders of men has conquered death? Philosophers, gurus and prophets all die. This fact mocks the noblest ambitions and aspirations of men. Yet there was One who died and rose again. The Lord Jesus came out of the tomb having destroyed "him that had the power of death, that is, the devil" (Heb 2:14). He claimed power over death when He said, "Therefore doth my Father love me, because I lay down my life, that I might take it again. No man taketh it from me, but I lay it down of myself. I have power to lay it down, and I have power to take it again. This commandment have I received of my Father" (John 10:17-18).

The resurrection appearances of the Lord Jesus were many and varied over a period of forty days. He appeared to various groups of people, at different times, and in different circumstances. Some of His appearances were behind closed doors, others out of doors along the road, by a lakeside and on a mountainside. Sometimes He appeared to individuals and at other times to groups varying in number from two to five hundred people. His appearances took place at different times of the day, some being early in the morning, others in early and late evening, and at least one at breaking of day. Why do the Scriptures record so many appearances, in varying circumstances, to different groups of people? At least one reason must surely have been to dispel the notion or idea that those who claimed to have seen Him may have been hallucinating. If there had been merely one or two sightings by the same people in similar circumstances, it would have looked suspiciously like a collective delusion, an example of powerful auto-suggestion or group hysteria. The resurrection appearances, because they are so numerous and so varied, cannot be rationalised as some kind of mass psychotic phenomenon.

Another possible notion is that the writers of scripture were deliberately setting out to deceive. The reader must make his or her own judgement as to whether Matthew, Mark, Luke, John, Paul, and Peter were capable of such a wicked conspiracy. The only explanation for the resurrection appearances is that Christ did in fact rise from the dead and appeared to many over a forty day period - "But now is Christ risen from the dead, and become the firstfruits of them that slept" (1 Cor 15:20). There is no one else who has broken the hold of death and conquered the tomb. The combined forces of science and philosophy cannot even prevent death, not to mention reversing and abolishing the process. In this, yet again, Christ stands alone and unique.

The importance of the *bodily* resurrection of Christ could not be over-stated. As already noted, it is the historical fact of His resurrection that validates the Bible. If Christ did not rise from the dead, then we can forget about all the other transcending claims of the Bible, and Christianity must take its place as a mere equal among the religions of the world. However, if in fact Christ has risen from the dead and lives today, then the Bible is assuredly true, and the so-called great faiths and religions of the world are necessarily of men and not of God. The concept of pluralism is therefore totally incompatible with the Bible and with the gospel of our Lord Jesus Christ.

New Age Spirituality

Pluralism rejects the claim of any one belief system to be uniquely and exclusively true. This has resulted in traditional Christian beliefs being abandoned in favour of many new kinds of religious experiment. We have already observed that in Paul's day, the ancient world was characterised by occult, pantheism, polytheism, idolatry, philosophy, and hedonism. It is evident that the wheel has gone full circle, and that the world today has returned to pagan nature worship and unnatural behaviour.

When Paul addressed the men of Athens, his Gentile audience was divided between Epicureans and Stoics.[34] We noted earlier that the Epicureans were atheistic, while the Stoics were pantheistic. This is remarkably similar to the division of postmodern society in our own age. There are those who, like the Epicureans, have a purely materialistic view of life, believing in non-purposive randomness and chance. But there are also those who, like the Stoics, believe that the world is an organic, living, rational, soul. In other words, Epicureanism is very similar to the atheistic side of postmodern philosophy, while Stoicism has much in common with New Age spirituality. There is truly nothing new under the sun! How relevant is the comment made by the Christian writer, Harry Ironside: "Every form of evil teaching now current was exposed by inspired writers in apostolic days."[35]

When we pay a visit to any large High Street bookstore, we are struck by the small shelf space allotted to "Christianity", in contrast to the huge collection of works displayed under "Mind, Body and Spirit". A multiplicity of books is available on such

---

[34] See pp.35-40.
[35] Ironside, H.A. *Epistles of John and Jude* (Loizeaux Brothers, NJ, repr. 1986) in Prefatory Note to Jude.

subjects as Earth Based Religions, Divination, Mythology, Druidism, Gaia, Native American, Shamanism, Witchcraft and Wicca, Magic, Satanism and Demonology, Astral Projection, Reincarnation, Spirit Guides and Guardian Angels, Nature Spirits and Elementals, Spirit Totoms, Archangels, Gods and Goddesses, Sixth Sense and Cosmic Consciousness, Gnosticism, and Astrology.

We do well to remind ourselves at this juncture that the Bible does not allow us to have any kind of involvement in the occult. God commanded the people of Israel, through Moses: "There shall not be found among you...that useth divination, or an observer of times, or an enchanter, or a witch, or a charmer, or a consulter with familiar spirits, or a wizard, or a necromancer. For all that do these things are an abomination unto the LORD" (Deut 18:10-12). Similarly, in the last book of the Bible, when John was given a vision of the Holy City, the New Jerusalem, he heard the One who sat on the throne say: "But the fearful, and unbelieving, and murderers, and whoremongers, and sorcerers, and idolators, and all liars, shall have their part in the lake which burneth with fire and brimstone: which is the second death" (Rev 21:8).

We shall therefore not delve into such subjects, for they are enemy territory. We recall the example set by those believers of Ephesus who renounced the magic arts they had once practised, by publicly burning their books (Acts 19:19). We do not need to know any more about the Devil than what the Bible tells us! However, what we can note is that all of these practices have one infernal lie in common, and that is their assertion of the deity of man. We are all part of the divine, so we are told, and salvation consists in discovering our divinity within.

If we were able to take Paul into a modern bookshop and show him the books available in the "Mind, Body and Spirit" section, would he be unfamiliar with the subject matter? Would it all be new and puzzling to him? The startling fact is that there is virtually nothing on offer today that Paul would not have met in one form or another in the ancient world. It was in Samaria, Cyprus and Ephesus, where Paul encountered magic and sorcery; in Philippi, he was confronted with divination; at Lystra, he witnessed the superstitious devotion to mythological gods; at Athens, he observed a city wholly given to idolatry; and at Ephesus, he saw the evil lure of goddess worship. New Age mysticism is a revival of the nature religions and occultism of the past.

The underlying philosophy of the New Age movement draws heavily from the ideas of neo-Paganism, Occult, Buddhism and Hinduism. New Age beliefs are a mixture of monism (all is one), and pantheism (all is God). In other words, all is one, all is god; and we are god. Men are divine, or potentially so, and do not need to be saved in any Bible sense of the term. We are asked to believe that man's problem is not his sin, but ignorance of his divinity. According to this teaching, "salvation is realizing balance or harmony with oneself, others, the earth, the god/ dess, the Divine Being".[36] We are told that man's need is not redemption, but enlightenment; his future hope is not resurrection, but reincarnation. Tapping into one's inner resources will bring knowledge, empowerment, a realization of infinite human potential, and an appreciation of one's own divinity. Thus the message of New Age is a repackaging of the first lie told by the serpent in the garden of Eden: "Ye shall not surely die: For God doth know that in the day ye eat thereof, then your eyes shall be opened, and *ye shall be as gods*, knowing good and evil" (Gen 3:4-5).

What does New Age say about the Person of Christ? The New Age movement speaks of 'Jesus' as an incarnation of the 'Christ principle'. They contend that He was one of many masters or avatars who are supposed to be periodic manifestations of Divinity. He is referred to as a 'cosmic Christ', and is placed in the pantheon of God-gurus, alongside Buddha, Krishna, Lao Tse and others. We are told He believed in the 'Fatherhood of God and the Brotherhood of Man'. Christ taught, according to New Age advocates, that every man has the Divine

---

[36] Hawkins, Craig S. *Goddess Worship, Witchcraft and Neo-Paganism* (OM Publishing, Zondervan, 1998) p.60.

within him, and that this Divinity is omnipresent. This, however, is nothing more than Hinduism.

How are we to judge the validity of religious teaching such as this? The criterion for judging all teaching is the *scriptural doctrine of Christ*. In other words, I must first judge a man by what he says about Christ, remembering that the doctrine of Christ is not negotiable. In his second letter, John advises the elect lady to judge every visiting preacher by his adherence to sound doctrine concerning Christ, "Whosoever transgresseth, and abideth not in the doctrine of Christ, hath not God. He that abideth in the doctrine of Christ, he hath both the Father and the Son. If there come any unto you, and bring not this doctrine, receive him not into your house, neither bid him God speed: for he that biddeth him God speed is partaker of his evil deeds" (2 John 9-11). There is no doubt whatever that the New Age movement is evil, demonic, and antichrist.

The very old heresy of Gnosticism has been revived and popularised in recent times largely by the writings of Elaine Pagels and Stuart Holroyd. The Gnostic, who takes side with the serpent, believes that the world was the work of an incompetent or malevolent deity. Gnosticism, which was a dualistic belief system, held that only spirit is good, while the material world and the human body are irredeemably evil. Salvation can only be by 'gnosis' or knowledge. However, when a Gnostic speaks of salvation, he does not mean salvation from sin, but from ignorance. He does not believe in redemption, but in the knowledge that redeems. To Gnostics, the idea of bodily resurrection is repugnant, for the body is part of the debased order of creation, and the Gnostic quest is to liberate the spirit from it.

The ideas of Gnosticism were a danger to the early church. Paul refutes the errors very clearly in his letter to the Colossians. The physical universe and the human body were not the work of a lesser incompetent deity, but the work of the Lord Jesus, "For by him were all things created, that are in heaven, and that are in earth, visible and invisible, whether they be thrones, or dominions, or principalities, or powers: all things were created by him, and for him: and he is before all things, and by him all things consist" (Col 1:16). Salvation is not by human knowledge, but by "redemption through his blood, even the forgiveness of sins" (Col 1:14). It is a false dualism that says that the spirit is good, while the body is evil. Matter, as such, is not evil. It is sin that is the problem, not the body. Paul wrote, concerning the incarnation of the Son of God, "For in him dwelleth all the fullness of the Godhead bodily" (Col 2:9). Concerning the resurrection of Christ, Paul wrote, "And he is the head of the body, the church: who is the beginning, the firstborn from the dead; that in all things he might have the pre-eminence" (Col 1:18). All believers ought to be very familiar with the Christ-exalting letter to the Colossians.

The danger today is that even genuine Christians can become influenced by New Age philosophy without being aware of it. New Age ideas are seldom presented in recognisably occult terms, but are usually packaged in benign and appealing language. For example, popular management books on sale in many outlets are often based on the ideas of the 'human potential' movement, a product of New Age philosophy. In the magazine *Professional Manager*[37] for May 2001, the audio books on offer included *Awaken the Giant Within* by Anthony Robbins, *The 7 Habits of Highly Effective People* by Stephen Covey, and *The Art of Happiness* by the Dalai Lama himself. The motto of the 'human potential' publishing house Nightingale Conant, is "You are what you think about". They send regular unsolicited mailshots advertising various audio courses which promise to transform one's life. One such offer, *Self Mastery*, which was mailed to my home address, was written by hypnotist Dick Sutphen. This course claimed that I could supercharge my subconscious mind, enjoy inner peace, live stress-free forever, enjoy a positive outlook, and always be in control. On a closer look, I discovered that what was on offer was a course in Zen, supposedly a combination of ancient wisdom and cutting-edge mind technology. The advertisement

---

[37] *Professional Manager* (Institute of Management, UK, Vol 10, Issue 3, May 2001).

assured me that I would achieve an altered state of consciousness almost immediately. Such claims and offers are a common feature of life today, and the Christian must to be able to recognise when there is 'death in the pot'.

The foundation of much of New Age thinking today was laid by the psychologist Abraham Maslow, the father of "self-actualisation." He developed the theory in his book *Toward a Psychology of Being*, published in 1968. Maslow compiled a hierarchy of needs in which he proposed that men had higher needs that could not be met until basic lower needs had been satisfied. Starting at the bottom of the pyramid, lower order needs were Physiological (food, clothes, shelter), and Security (freedom from danger). The higher order needs were Social (need for others), Esteem (need to be held in high regard), and, at the top of the pyramid, Self-actualisation (maximisation of one's potential). The new religious quest of life has become this self-centred goal of self-actualisation. According to business writer, Martha Nichols, the 1980's were all about style and lifestyle, whereas the 1990's were about soul-searching and meaning.[38] The business world has realised that there is a spiritual thirst in man. No one wants to think that his or her life is meaningless. The New Age message is that this thirst can be satisfied, not by Christ, but by self-actualisation. This, we are assured, is the equivalent of "getting in touch with your authentic self". The commercial marketers have not been slow to exploit the business potential of the new creed.

D.A.Carson has helpfully written, "The more I read the New Age literature, the more I am struck by several facts. Almost none of it seriously wrestles with the historical and textual arguments put forward by serious Christians. New Age thought is insufferably fuzzy and inconsistent. Anything it likes or can use, it rips out of its historic context and redeploys with new content, often made out of whole cloth. It almost never deals with evil, because it is most commonly pantheistic - and

---

[38] Nichols, Martha "Does New Age Business Have a Message for Managers?" in *Harvard Business Review* (Harvard University, Boston, March-April 1994) p.52.

religions that do not wrestle with the problems of human evil are blind beyond words. Worse, almost all of this multiplying thought is irremediably selfish. The aim of the exercise is self-fulfilment, self-actualisation, serenity, productivity, power. God, if he/she/it exists, exists for me. And from a biblical perspective, it is this profound selfishness that lies at the heart of all human sin."[39]

As well as 'human potential' books, there are also harmless looking and attractively produced publications about alternative therapies, holistic health, and meditation, which are actually occultist in nature. The enormous popularity of Yoga is a case in point. Yoga classes are available everywhere, with classes for both children and adults. What is Yoga, and is it harmless? One ignores the philosophical side of Yoga at their peril. The common perception of Yoga is that it is merely a system of physical exercises and breathing control, whereas in reality it is a Hindu system of meditation and self-control designed to produce mystical experience and spiritual insight.[40] The aim is to induce an altered state of consciousness, in order to become aware of one's union with God or ultimate reality. Like all occult practices, Yoga is potentially very harmful.

It is vital to see a distinction between 'meditation' as spoken of in the Bible, and the 'meditation' of Eastern and New Age mysticism. We strongly advise any believer to have nothing to do with Yoga. Eastern style meditation involves emptying the mind and inducing a trance-like state of altered consciousness. By contrast, Biblical meditation is the employment of a sanctified mind in conscious and intelligent thought upon the Word of God. No one worships God in a trance or in a state of altered consciousness. Paul told the Corinthian believers that spiritual worship engages the conscious mind: "I will pray with the spirit, and I will pray with the *understanding* also: I will sing with the spirit, and I will sing with the *understanding* also"

---

[39] Carson, D.A. *The Gagging of God - Christianity confronts Pluralism* (Apollos, IVP, Leicester, England, 1996) p.331.
[40] Ankerberg, John & Weldon, John *Encyclopedia of New Age Beliefs* (Harvest House, Oregon, 1996) p.595.

(1 Cor 14:15). Even in the days when 'prophecy' was still a current gift, Paul said, "And the spirits of the prophets are subject to the prophets" (v.32). In other words, the prophets had conscious self-control at all times. For purposes of Christian meditation, the Bible informs us on the kind of subject matter that should occupy our minds. Paul advises the Philippians: "Finally, brethren, whatsoever things are true, whatsoever things are honest, whatsoever things are just, whatsoever things are pure, whatsoever things are lovely, whatsoever things are of good report; if there be any virtue, and if there be any praise, *think on these things*" (Phil 4:8).

In the scientific fields of physics and biology, New Age thinkers have abandoned the Enlightenment's mechanistic view of life, in favour of an organic, self-organising world. In recent times, John Lovelock has popularised the idea of Gaia (from the Greek goddess of earth). In the Preface to his book *Gaia*[41], Lovelock writes, "the biosphere is a self-regulating entity with the capacity to keep our planet healthy by controlling the chemical and physical environment." In other words, the earth itself acts like a single organism. Gaians believe that the earth is a living, breathing being, and that creatures, rivers, oceans, mountains, forests and prairies are part of that being. According to this theory, we are inescapably connected to one another via all the earth's systems. This monistic (all is one) view of the universe is also espoused in other works, such as Capra's best-selling book *The Tao of Physics*.[42]

The improbability of Darwinian evolution has not been lost on New Age thinkers. The ideas of Sir Fred Hoyle have been eagerly claimed as supportive of their pantheistic position. In his book *The Intelligent Universe*, Hoyle asks us to imagine a blindfolded person trying to solve the Rubik cube. The chances against achieving perfect colour matching are about 50,000,000,000,000,000,000 to 1. Hoyle points out that these odds are roughly the same as those against just one of our body's

---

[41] Lovelock, James E. *Gaia* (Oxford University Press, 1979).
[42] Capra, Fritjof *The Tao of Physics* (Wildwood House, London, 1975).

200,000 proteins having evolved randomly, by chance. The idea of life originating in an organic soup on earth is, for Hoyle, untenable. Hoyle is right thus far, but unfortunately, his alternative suggestion is equally as foolish. Hoyle proposes a 'cosmic theory' that life came to earth from outer space. Further, concluding that life must have originated by design rather than accident, Hoyle proposes a pantheistic explanation: "The intelligence responsible for the creation of carbon-based life in the cosmic theory is firmly *within* the universe and is subservient to it. Because the creator of carbon-based life was not all-powerful, there is consequently no paradox in the fact that terrestrial life is far from ideal."[43] Hoyle, who describes himself as 'unrepentantly Greek', has rejected the Biblical revelation of a transcendent Creator, in favour of deity and intelligence lying within the universe. Hoyle, like many others, is worshipping the creation rather than the Creator. If Hoyle had been in Athens when Paul was preaching, he would undoubtedly have been standing among the Stoics.

It is interesting to observe the challenge that other Gaian scientists have made to traditional Darwinian evolution. The Gaian writer, Charles Birch, has stated, "Evolution raises a profound question: Why did atoms evolve into cells and into plants and animals? Why didn't creativity stop with the first DNA molecule? Mechanism provides no answer. The ecological model opens up ways to explore in terms of lure and response, or purposive influence and self-determination."[44] Thus mechanism is rejected in favour of ecology. The atheistic/mechanistic view is set aside, not for a Creator/creationist view, but for a pantheistic/ecological view.

The postmodernist claims that no standpoint of thought is uniquely privileged above other standpoints. In the religious realm, this approach has become known as pluralism. But the same approach is also applied to science. We are now told that modern science has no special claims to truth, for it is as much

---

[43] Hoyle, Sir Fred *The Intelligent Universe* (Michael Joseph, London, 1983) p.236.
[44] Birch, Charles "The Postmodern Challenge to Biology" in *The Post-Modern Reader* Ed. Charles Jencks (Academy Editions, London) p.397.

of a cultural construct of the West as other sciences are of their cultures. Faith in modern science, for the postmodernist, is only a sign of Eurocentrism and cultural imperialism. Meera Nanda, who is a firm believer in the Enlightenment approach to science, has warned, "For a postmodernist, other cultures are under no rational obligation to revise their cosmologies, or adopt new procedures for ascertaining facts to bring them in accord with modern science."[45] Alarmed at the acceptance in British schools of Vedic science as promoted today by Hindu propagandists, Nanda has written:

"One of the most ludicrous mantras of Hindutva propaganda is that there is "no conflict" between modern science and Hinduism. In reality, everything we know about the workings of nature through the methods of modern science radically disconfirms the presence of any morally significant gunas, or shakti, or any other form of consciousness in nature, as taught by the Vedic cosmology which treats nature as a manifestation of divine consciousness. Far from there being "no conflict" between science and Hinduism, a scientific understanding of nature completely and radically negates the "eternal laws" of Hindu dharma which teach an identity between spirit and matter. That is precisely why the Hindutva apologists are so keen to tame modern science by reducing it to "simply another name for the One Truth" - the "one truth" of Absolute Consciousness contained in Hinduism's own classical texts."

Another Gaian thinker, Edward Goldsmith, has pointed out that neither Darwinism, nor the neo-Darwinism of Bateson and Weissman, nor its latest version, the Synthetic Theory, provides an evolutionary theory that is recognisable with our knowledge of the structure and function of the world of living things. Goldsmith maintains that little attempt has been made to provide any serious evidence for the Darwinian theory, and that this has been noted by a number of critics, including Karl Popper, who consider that neither Darwin nor any Darwinian

---

[45] Nanda, Meera *Prophets Facing Backward: Postmodern Critiques of Science and Hindu Nationalism in India* (Rutgers University Press, 2003)

has so far given an actual causal explanation of the adaptive evolution of any single organism or any single organ. Goldsmith goes on to give glory to the creation rather than the Creator: "According to the Gaia thesis, the biosphere, together with the atmospheric environment, forms a single entity or natural system. This system is the product of organic forces that are highly coordinated by the system itself. Gaia has, in effect, created herself, not in a random manner but in a goal-directed manner since the system is highly stable and is capable of maintaining its stability in the face of internal and external challenges. It is, in fact, a cybernetic system, and for this to be possible, Gaia must display considerable order, indeed, she must be seen as a vast cooperative enterprise, very much as nature was seen by the Natural Theologians of the nineteenth century."[46]   Again, the truth of the transcendent Creator is denied in favour of a self-creating, self-organising universe.

The reader might well be wondering where he has heard something like this before. Is the idea of a self-organising, organic world, a new belief? Not in the least! Paul was already familiar with such ideas, for they were held by the Stoic pantheists of Athens. Rejecting the materialistic atomism of Epicurus, the Stoic viewed life as a kind of continuum, and saw the world itself as an organic, living, rational soul. Today, the New Age devotees reject the mechanistic world of the atheist, and view it instead as a living organism. A recent book popularising the teachings of the Stoic philosopher, Seneca, claims that "Stoicism was a 'New Age' philosophy for the third century BC".[47] Stoicism is being revived and marketed as a philosophy eminently suitable for the postmodern world.

What should be the Christian's response to New Age thought? We have seen that the two prevailing non-Christian worldviews today are those of mechanistic materialism and animistic pantheism. These worldviews correspond closely to

---

[46] Goldsmith, Edward "Gaia and Evolution" in *The Post-Modern Reader* Ed. Charles Jencks (Academy Editions, London) p.399.
[47] Forstater, Mark & Radin, Victoria *The Spiritual Teachings of Seneca - Ancient Philosophy for Modern Wisdom* (Coronet Books, Hodder & Stoughton, London, 2001) p.63.

the Epicureanism and Stoicism of the ancient world. We have already noted how Paul preached to these two groupings at Athens. He pointed to the transcendent Creator and His creation, and to the risen Lord Jesus Christ whom God has appointed as the future Judge of the world. We should do the same.

Hyperreality and the Power of Myth

In the mid-1990s, it was reported in the British press that more people in Great Britain were taking their religious inspiration from *Star Wars* than from church services. George Lucas, the creator of the series, not only wrote an epic science fiction story, but also invented a fictional religion. David Wilkinson has pointed out that *Star Wars* unashamedly introduced spirituality into its central themes, exemplified by the Jedi's reliance on the Force.[48] In the films, the famous line "May the Force be with you" taps into an energy field that is supposedly created by all living things. This Force surrounds us, penetrates us, and binds the galaxy together. Although the idea of the Force was created for the make-believe world of *Star Wars*, its underlying philosophy is borrowed from the ancient Chinese philosophy of Tao. According to this philosophy, Tao is a force that pervades the universe, is the source of the universe, and *is* the universe. Lucas re-invented the impersonal, rational god of Stoicism and Eastern mysticism, and called it the Force. People have believed in the Force in typical postmodern fashion, not because they believe it is actually true, but because it caters to their own idea of God. This is an example of man creating a god in his own image, a god who is non-threatening and who does not judge sin. *They have believed a fiction, while knowing it to be a fiction!* Men who believe a myth, while knowing it to be a myth, have truly become fools.

The postmodern mindset asserts that all meaning, truth and

---

[48] Wilkinson, David *The Power of the Force - The Spirituality of the Star Wars Films* (Lion Publishing plc, Oxford, 2000) p.35.

purpose are man-made. The distinction has been lost between fact and fiction, between truth and myth. The 'real' has been subsumed by the 'hyperreal'. This postmodern phenomenon can be seen in the proliferation of theme parks, virtual reality and computer games. What had been simulation has now become 'real'. We live in a culture where 'image' is more important than 'content'. This idea of hyperreality was first propounded by the French philosopher Jean Baudrillard (1929). I take the liberty of quoting my past Professor on Baudrillard's observations.

"According to Jean Baudrillard, the much-vaunted high priest of postmodernism, the condition of postmodernity is perhaps best portrayed as a milieu in which there is more and more information but less and less meaning, where everything is commodified and subject to the demands of the market, and in which the production, distribution and manipulation of *image* - the 'political economy of the sign' - is all-important. Postmodernity is a depthless world of simulation, where images bear no discernible relationship to external reality and where artifice, in the words of the postmodern rock group U2, is 'even better than the real thing'. Nowhere is this tendency better illustrated than in Disneyland, which in many respects is more authentic in its authenticity than the surrounding environment because Disneyland at least acknowledges its artificiality. For Baudrillard, indeed, Disneyland has been created as imaginary in order to make us believe that the rest is real, to disguise the fact that the rest of Los Angeles is no longer real but a simulation. In postmodernity, therefore, the 'real' world has imploded into a state of hyperreality, a hallucinogenic simulation of the non-existent, a place where boundaries collapse, opposites coalesce, fact and fiction are fused, and theory and practice metamorphose."[49]

Baudrillard certainly makes some insightful observations about the postmodern condition. People are feeding their minds on unreality. By far the single most dominant influence on

---

[49] Brown, Stephen *Postmodern Marketing* (Routledge, 1995) p.80.

society in recent times has been that of television. This form of media has pervaded the lives of all but a tiny minority. Television audiences are fixated by soaps and chat shows, while serious issues are trivialised. Baudrillard said, "Television knows no night. It is perpetual day. TV embodies our fear of the dark, of night, of the other side of things." For postmodern society, television facilitates the ultimate escapism into a world of make-believe. People are beginning to lose the distinction between true science and science fiction, between Physics and *Star Trek,* between real life and soap. The obsession with image rather than content is attributable in large measure to television. The death of the book, and the rise of television, are greatly to be lamented. Watching television is radically different to reading a book. It has been observed that pictures need to be recognised, whereas words need to be understood. Neil Postman has said, "Pictures present the world as objects, language presents the world as ideas".[50] We are raising a new generation of video-dependent children, for whom the meaning of life is merely fun and relaxation.

The negative influence of television is now being compounded by those other marvels of modern technology: the internet and computer games. Quite apart from the evil material that one can easily access, the internet has brought a world of information and knowledge within all our reach. This, of course, is both good and bad. We no longer need go to the library to open a book, find the place, and read the passage. Within seconds of going on-line, we can have a massive overload of information on almost any subject of our choosing. However, this quantum increase in knowledge and information does not appear to help us to think any more seriously about reality. Undoubtedly, the internet can be used profitably for serious research, but it also makes it easier to feed our fantasies in a virtual world of unreality.

What are we to say to a generation for whom myth has

---

[50] Cited in Brown, William E. "Theology in a Postmodern Culture: Implications of a Video-Dependent Society" in *The Challenge of Postmodernism,* p.318.

become the truth, and for whom fiction has become fact? Without doubt, this generation needs to hear about reality and truth as presented in the Bible. The Lord Jesus said "I am the way, the truth, and the life: no man cometh unto the Father, but by me" (John 14:6). This is reality. The postmodern man no longer asks, "Does God exist?" but "Which God?" The answer must come with all the authority of Scripture - God does exist, but He is neither Allah, nor Buddha, nor Krishna, nor the universe. He is the living God of the Bible, the God and Father of our Lord Jesus Christ. There *is* meaning to life and history, there *is* a judgement, there *is* the need of personal faith in Christ, there *is* forgiveness of sins as offered in the gospel, and there *is* a Saviour.

Morality and Gender

The concept of Bible-based morality has been exchanged for the new creed of moral relativism. I recently sat with five business colleagues and listened to a Sales Person selling the merits of her company's health insurance. The young lady advised us that not only could employees of the company benefit from this particular insurance scheme, but our partners could also benefit. Then, without hesitation or embarrassment, she qualified the word 'partner' by explaining that it applied to husbands and wives, live-in partners, and same-sex partners. It struck me as quite a commentary on life today. Society has abandoned the God-given, creatorial order of relationships, and has accepted 'life styles' which are unnatural and abnormal, immoral and amoral, sinful and ungodly. Such things are no longer the secrets of the night, but are openly flaunted as normal and politically correct.

What has been happening to society? The foundations of society, such as the institution of marriage and family, are being dismantled and destroyed. During a recent Synod of the Church of England, a *Times* reporter Alan Hamilton wrote, "So occupied is the Anglican community with the homosexuality debate that the issue has generated its own shorthand, with one speaker from the floor referring to 'LGBT Christians.' That's lesbians, gays, bisexuals and transsexuals. We haven't left anyone out, have we?"[51] Postmodernism is by nature anti-foundational. The result is moral chaos.

Regarding the anti-foundationalism of postmodernism, Veith in his excellent book has this to say, "The great intellectual systems of the past (such as Platonism; Christianity; Marxism; Science) have always had specific foundations (rational ideals; God; economics; empirical observation). Postmodernism, on the other hand, is anti-foundational. It seeks to destroy all such objective foundations and to replace them with nothing."[52] We now live in a postmodern culture which tolerates same-sex marriage, and which has legalised the adoption of children by same-sex couples. And should we raise our voice in protest against this state of affairs, we are told that the problem is not homosexuality, but homophobia.

This anti-foundationalism can also be seen in the rise of feminism. No study of postmodernity would be complete without considering the issue of gender. A social revolution has taken place that has changed the 'traditional' role of women in society. The distinction between male and female has been largely compromised in terms of appearance and dress. The feminist movement has made its mark socially, politically, and theologically. Socially, women today are under enormous pressure to put a personal career before their family. Feminism has done a great disservice to women, by making them feel that to stay at home and raise a family is somehow inferior and demeaning. Home life and family life have suffered greatly as a result.

Theologically, feminism has wreaked havoc with scriptural truth. Daphne Hampson, typical of postmodern feminist theologians, discards Christianity as both untrue and unethical. Hampson claims: "With the coming of modernity in the eighteenth century, it (Christianity) became untenable. Christians, in part, recognise this. They have in succession

---

[51] Hamilton, Alan reporting in *The Times,* Thursday, February 12, 2004, p.4.
[52] Veith, Gene Edward *Guide to Contemporary Culture* (Crossway Books, Leicester, 1994) p.48.

discarded the literal meaning of Genesis, then the virgin birth, now many discount the resurrection as a flesh-and-blood event. However they have sought to move sideways, saying that although it is not true, Christianity may be retained as a 'true myth'. What has happened with the rise of feminism is that this has become unavailable. Feminism has made it evident that Christianity, far from being a true or helpful myth, is a profoundly harmful myth. It has served, and still serves today, to legitimise the inferior place of women in society. The Christian myth now appears as a projection of patriarchy, calculated to justify a patriarchal order to both women and men."[53]

For the Bible-believing Christian, the most obnoxious teaching of recent times has been the feminist idea that God is both male and female. Gender-free translations of the Bible have begun to appear on the bookshelves. It is now common to hear God referred to as 'she'. In its most extreme form, this trend toward matriarchalism has led to a revival of interest in ancient goddess-worshipping religions. New Age neo-pagans have rejected the idea of Father-God in favour of Mother-earth. This movement strikes at the heart of God's creatorial order. The scriptural language concerning the 'gender' of God is always stated in the masculine. He is the God and Father of our Lord Jesus Christ. To speak of God as if He were a god/goddess is blasphemy of the worst kind. Yet it has been necessary to mention these things to show to what extent society has gone in its rejection of Christian foundations.

In the Bible, the role of the woman is that of a loving and caring helper to the man. The man is to love and cherish his wife as his own body, while the wife is to love and respect her husband (Eph 5:22-33). There is to be mutual consideration for one another in all areas of marriage (1 Cor 7:3-5). If all married couples were to practise these divine injunctions, there would be no marriage breakdowns, no divorce, and no need for marriage counsellors. The great God-given role for the woman

---

[53] Hampson, Daphne *After Christianity* (SCM Press Ltd, 1966).

is to be the homemaker (1 Tim 5:14). In spite of prevailing feminist and liberal ideas, we should be clear that in marriage, the husband is the head of the wife as Christ is the head of the church (Eph 5:23). Equally, when believers are gathered together as a church, the same creatorial order must be observed. The women, who are commanded by scripture to remain silent, must cover their heads in recognition of the headship of the men, while the men are to keep their heads uncovered in recognition of the headship of Christ (1 Cor 11:1-16). This order, when observed within a local church gathering, is both scriptural and Christ-honouring. These truths have been lost almost without trace in mainstream Christendom.

Globalisation

There is yet another feature of postmodernity that we must consider before closing this study, and it is that of globalisation. For the greater part of the twentieth century, a man's worldview was said to be limited by a Euro-American centrism. Today the postmodern mindset has replaced this with the idea of globalism. The world is now seen as a global village, not only in terms of economy and trade, but also in terms of political and religious ethos. The world has many ethnic, cultural and religious differences within it, and the new postmodern global society is perceived as multi-cultural and multi-faith. All religions and cultures are looked upon as 'true' in the subjective and local sense. No one religion is permitted to be true in the exclusive, objective and absolute sense. Globalism and pluralism are marks of the postmodern world of unbelief.

Philosophy and religion can sometimes appear in the most unlikely places. In my secular employment, I am involved in the marketing and selling of precast concrete products. I try to keep abreast of developments within the industry by reading trade journals and magazines. I was not a little surprised to find an article about religion in a concrete technology magazine published in Germany. An address had been given to the German Concrete Society by the theologian,

Hans Kung.[54]   He informed his audience that the "Council of the Parliament of World Religions", which met in Chicago in 1993, was attended by 6,500 representatives from all kinds of religions. Hans Kung reported that for the first time in the history of religion, a declaration on a world ethos had been agreed, with Kung having been responsible for drawing up the declaration. Explaining what he meant by a world ethos, Kung explained:

"A global ethos is not a new ideology or superstructure; its aim is not to make the specific ethos of the different religions and philosophies superfluous; it is thus no substitute for the Torah, the Sermon on the Mount, the Koran, the Bhagavad-Gita, the words of Buddha or the sayings of Confucius. The single world ethos does not mean a single world culture and certainly not a single world religion. Put in positive terms: A global ethos, a world ethos is nothing else than the necessary minimum of common human values, standards and basic attitudes. Or more precisely: The world ethos is the basic consensus in respect of binding values, irrevocable standards and basic attitudes which can be accepted by all religions despite their dogmatic differences and also supported by non-believers."

Kung's *Chicago Declaration* is a typically postmodern, pluralist, globalist document. This should ring alarm bells with every true, Bible-believing Christian[55]. This is putting our Lord Jesus Christ on the same level as Moses, Mohammed, Krishna, Buddha and Confucius. But who can doubt that this global ethos is preparing the hearts and minds of men for that culmination of unbelief and rebellion against God, when "that man of sin be revealed, the son of perdition; who opposeth and exalteth himself above all that is called God, or that is worshipped; so that he as God sitteth in the temple of God, shewing himself that he is God" (2 Thess 2:3-4)?

---

[54] Kung, Hans, "Without a World Ethos there can be no Better World Order" in *Concrete Precasting Plant and Technology,* Issue 5/1997 (*Betonwerk + Fertigteil-Technik,* Wiesbaden, Germany).

[55] A further meeting of the Parliament of the World's Religions was held July 7-14 in Barcelona in 2004, attended by 8600 participants from over 70 countries, and was hailed as a great success.

Conclusion

We have seen that postmodernism is a philosophical movement which not only rejects Biblical revelation, but also opposes the Enlightenment ideas of objective truth and human progress. In other words, there can be no universal rationality or theory of knowledge. Postmodernism claims that truth is relative rather than absolute; temporal rather than eternal; ethnic rather than universal; pluralist rather than exclusive; fragmented rather than unified.

We remind the reader that the assumptions of postmodernism are illogical and self-defeating. We summarise three such contradictions:

1) The postmodernist states that there is no such thing as absolute truth. But the statement, by its own definition, cannot itself be true in any absolute sense and cannot therefore be applied universally. In other words, to state in absolute terms that there is no such thing as absolute truth, is self-contradictory nonsense.

2) The relativist notion that truth is purely subjective leads to the conclusion that two or more materially different and contradictory beliefs can each be true, even though they might be mutually exclusive. Thus subjectivism and relativism violate the Non-Contradiction Principle, that *A cannot be non-A*.

3) The post-structuralist writer Derrida asserted that a literary text can only be interpreted subjectively by the reader. What did Derrida mean when he wrote this? It doesn't matter, because we are not allowed to ask. The reader makes the meaning, not the author. When we apply this rule to the writings of the post-structuralists themselves, we must disregard any meaning they may have intended. We can each impose our own meanings. Thus the practice of writing in verbalised propositional form, which is the very building block of language and logic, is reduced to an absurdity.

As we can see, the premises of postmodernism are therefore self-contradictory and self-referentially inconsistent. The foolishness of postmodernism is not new, but is the inevitable destination of a human journey which began when men exchanged the truth about God for a lie, and worshipped and served the creation rather than the Creator (Rom 1:25). As I have read and researched for the writing of this book, I have been startled by the similarities of today's major belief systems with those of the ancient world. It would seem that there have always been three main worldviews:

First, the atheistic/mechanistic view - In this first group are the Epicurean atheists, and their philosophical heirs, the secular humanists and the postmodernists. The Epicurean/atheistic position sees life as a chance phenomenon, caused by random and non-purposive processes, which can be explained in purely mathematical-mechanistic terms. This view holds that there is no God and no life after death. In that respect, today's postmodernism has much in common with Enlightenment modernism. Whereas modernism asserted that there was universal truth to be discovered, postmodernism claims that all notions of meaning, value or purpose, are only 'true' in the subjective, constructed, and man-made sense. Postmodernism is what you arrive at when you draw the non-Christian presuppositions of Epicureanism and modernism to their logical conclusions. You are left with emptiness, meaninglessness, and lostness. Gene Veith has written, "Modernist heresies have floundered, but now postmodernist heresies replace them. Rationalism, having failed, is giving way to irrationalism - both are hostile to God's revelation, but in different ways. Modernists did not believe the Bible is true. Postmodernists have cast out the category of truth altogether. In doing so, they have opened up a Pandora's Box of New Age religions, syncretism, and moral chaos."[56]

Second, the animistic/pantheistic view - In this second group are the Stoics, Hindus, Buddhists, Taoists, and Gnostics. Today's New Age spirituality is a descendant of the Stoic pantheism that Paul encountered in Athens. They did not believe that God created the universe, but rather that God *is* the universe. In other words, everything is part of God, and that includes us.

---

[56] Veith, Gene Edward *Guide to Contemporary Culture* (Crossway Books, Leicester, 1994) p.192.

According to this view, the universe is one, and is a self-organising array of interconnected energy fields, while the world is a single, living, unified, organism. This universal living energy is known by the Stoics as 'wisdom'; by the Eastern thinkers as 'Tao' or 'Ch'i'; by the New Age as 'Gaia'; and by *Star Wars* fans as the 'Force'. Like the Stoic pantheists, the New Age followers worship the creation, rather than the Creator.

Third, the Creator/creation view - There is a transcendent Creator who made the universe from nothing. God is not part of the universe, but is distinct from it and is infinitely above it. Included in this third group is the original Mosaic Judaism of the Old Testament, and of course, Christianity as revealed in the New Testament. It is the Bible, and the Bible alone, which reveals to us the truth about God and creation, as well as the purpose and meaning of human life. It is also in the Bible that we learn about Christ's deity and His sinless life, atoning death, resurrection, exaltation, and second advent. Further, it is in the Bible where we read about sin, guilt, repentance, faith in Christ, forgiveness, and eternal life.

Although the Creator/creation view is true in accordance with the Bible, there are sadly many strange birds that have lodged in the branches of this great tree. Belief systems which purportedly subscribe to the Creator/creation view, but who are in serious error, include modern Judaism and Islam. Again, we must judge such religions by their doctrine of Christ. For example, what do Judaism and Islam say about the death and resurrection of Christ? Modern Judaism says that Christ died, but that He did not rise again, while Islam claims that Christ didn't really die. The Bible, on the other hand, asserts that Christ both died and rose again, "For I delivered unto you first of all that which I also received, how that Christ died for our sins according to the scriptures; and that he was buried, and that he rose again the third day according to the scriptures..."(1 Cor 15:3-4).

In this chapter we have seen that the postmodern agenda is anti-foundationalist, in that it strikes at the foundations of Christianity and revealed truth. How then should we respond to this massive assault upon our faith? There can only be one response, and that is the faithful preaching of the gospel, combined with holy, separated living unto God. We are not asked to change the world, but we are commanded to "preach the gospel" (Mark 16:15), and to "contend for the faith which was once delivered unto the saints" (Jude 3). In our concluding chapter we shall revisit the gospel and draw some lessons for preaching the truth to a postmodern generation.

CHAPTER 7

The Unknown God

This book has been written with the purpose of helping Christians, and hopefully some non-Christians, to understand the nature of the changes going on around us. It is aimed, in particular, at young Christian students who will be confronted with postmodern philosophy in the course of their education. It is also intended for the older generation. Whether one is a gospel preacher, Sunday-school teacher, or Christian parent, it is vital that we are aware of the unbiblical ideas that our children, and our neighbours' children, may be imbibing from today's schools, universities, churches, press and media. The Western world has reached a moment in history when the rising generation is largely biblically illiterate. The God of the Bible has once again become the "unknown God" of Acts 17. It is now the duty and privilege of today's Christians to address our generation as Paul addressed the men of his generation in Athens: "Whom therefore ye ignorantly worship, him declare I unto you" (Acts 17:23). How can we do this in practical terms?

The first thing that we must note is that the gospel has not changed in any way. In fact, today's twenty-first century objections to the gospel do not differ materially from the first century objections with which Paul had to contend. This is good news for the concerned Christian, in that the answers to modernism and postmodernism are already in the Bible for us. There can be no other gospel. Paul instructed Timothy to charge the Ephesian believers that they might "teach no other doctrine" (1 Tim 1:3). We shall draw our conclusions with that divine injunction in mind.

The core message of the gospel cannot change, but our *starting point* can change to suit the needs of the person we are speaking to. This is amply demonstrated in the Bible. For example, the Lord Jesus spoke to Nicodemus in a different way to how He spoke to the woman of Samaria. Similarly, the apostles took one approach when preaching to Jews, and another approach when preaching to Gentiles. When preaching to Jews, the apostles began with the scriptures, and showed from them how it was necessary that Christ should suffer. That was the starting point. It was different for Gentiles, seeing that they had no knowledge of the scriptures and knew nothing about Christ. Therefore the starting point for Gentiles was the nature and character of God. For example, Paul urged the idolaters of Lystra to turn to the "living God, who made heaven, and earth, and sea" (Acts 14:15); he pointed the Greek philosophers to the "God that made the world, and all things therein" (Acts 17:24); and he reminded the Thessalonian believers that they had turned "from idols to serve the living and true God" (1 Thess 1:9). The starting point for our own postmodern generation must surely be the nature and character of God. He is the living, true, infinite, personal, God of the Bible. He is the eternal, sovereign, transcendent God of creation. He is a God of grace, love, peace, holiness, righteousness, mercy, longsuffering, goodness, faithfulness, kindness and joy. And, best of all, He is the God and Father of our Lord Jesus Christ. What a starting point!

Once again, let us remind ourselves of the core errors of today's prevailing philosophy. Postmodernism claims that truth is relative rather than absolute; temporal rather than eternal; ethnic rather than universal; pluralist rather than exclusive; fragmented rather than unified. The postmodern agenda therefore is anti-foundationalist, striking at the foundations of Christian doctrine and revealed truth.

Relative or Absolute?

What is truth? When Pilate asked that question of the Lord Jesus, unfortunately he did not wait for the answer (John 18:38).

The Lord had been telling Pilate that the very purpose of His birth and mission into this world was to bear witness to the truth. If only Pilate's question had been sincere! Let us, with sincerity, consider what the scriptures say about truth.

The Bible speaks of the reality that lies behind both the universe and human existence. The Old Testament begins with the primary revelation of truth: "In the beginning God created the heaven and the earth" (Gen 1:1). The New Testament revelation adds to this truth, "In the beginning was the Word, and the Word was with God, and the Word was God" (John 1:1). Behind our world and human existence, there is the triune God of the Bible. This is true in the absolute, universal, objective, and eternal sense. It is true and certain whether we believe it or not. We reject the postmodern answer that all truth is a man-made, relative term with no absolute dimension.

When we speak of God, we are not referring to some pantheistic notion of impersonal nature or force. It is vital to make a distinction between the Creator and the creation. God is not the universe, but He is the Creator of the universe. Further, He has created all things through His Son: "All things were made by him; and without him was not anything made that was made" (John 1:3). The truth is that God is the Creator of all things. Happily for us, He is also the Saviour of men. Paul made this clear when he wrote, "God our Saviour; will have all men to be saved and to come unto the knowledge of the truth" (1 Tim 2:3-4). What is the truth that God wants all to know? The Lord Jesus addressed His Father as the "only true God" (John 17:3). Therefore, when preaching or witnessing to our generation, we need to emphasise, and re-emphasise, the truth about God. Further, He wants all to come to a personal knowledge of Jesus Christ as Saviour and Lord.

If we believe the Bible to be the inerrant word of God, which we surely do, then we can reasonably expect that the Bible's teaching on the human condition will be fully consistent with our actual observations of the world around us. We confidently affirm that such is the case. Speaking of the Bible, the Lord Jesus said, "thy word is truth" (John 17:17). We have a divinely inspired book that tells us the truth about creation, human guilt, and salvation. These truths are not culturally conditioned constructs, but are truths for all men everywhere. We can tell a biblically illiterate generation that the Bible is the unchanging and unerring Word of God. We should freely teach, preach, and quote the Word of God. Paul reminded Timothy "from a child thou hast known the holy scriptures, which are able to make thee wise unto salvation through faith which is in Christ Jesus" (2 Tim 3:15).

Speaking of Himself, the Lord Jesus said "I am the way, the truth, and the life: no man cometh unto the Father but by me" (John 14:6). The Lord Jesus is the truth in the sense that all that can be known about God is seen in Him. All the fullness of God resides in Him. He is the perfect expression of God, and the brightness of His glory. He is God's well beloved Son, and His only begotten Son. He is "Jesus the Son of God" (Heb 4:14). John closed his first letter with the words: "And we know that the Son of God is come, and hath given us an understanding, that we may know him that is true, and we are in him that is true, even in his Son Jesus Christ. This is the true God, and eternal life" (1 John 5:20). This is truth in the absolute sense.

Temporal or Eternal?

Truth is not only absolute as opposed to relative, but is eternal as opposed to temporal. We need to appreciate that God has always existed, and that He always will exist. Moses fully appreciated the eternal being of God: "Before the mountains were brought forth, or ever thou hadst formed the earth and the world, even from *everlasting to everlasting*, thou art God" (Psalm 90:2). He is eternal, and His character never changes. God will always be holy, righteous, faithful, gracious, merciful, and loving.

Further, our decision in life concerning Christ will have an eternal outcome. Whether I am a Christian or not, will not only matter in this life, but will determine my destiny in eternity. The Bible says, "He that believeth on the Son hath everlasting life: and he that believeth not the Son shall not see life; but the wrath of God abideth on him" (John 3:36). The Bible speaks of events that happened before the foundation of the world, and of others which have happened from or since the foundation of the world. The Bible also points us to eternity, when death and hell will have been cast into the lake of fire, and the first heaven and the first earth will have passed away. John tells of his vision of the new heaven and the new earth, and the holy city, new Jerusalem, coming down from God out of heaven, prepared as a bride adorned for her husband (Rev 21:1-2). The throne of God and of the Lamb shall be in it, and his servants shall serve Him, and they shall see his face, and reign for ever and ever (Rev 22:3-5). When communicating the gospel by whatever means, we must emphasise the eternal import of the message. The truth of the Bible is absolute and eternal.

Ethnic or Universal?

Is the Christian gospel equally applicable to Bedouin Arabs, North American Indians, Kalahari Bushmen, and Amazon Indians? Should these indigenous peoples be left alone with their traditional beliefs? The anthropologists will tell us that ethnic religions should be protected from Christian missionaries. Indeed, it would seem that the maxim is "Ethnic is right, ethnic is better." It is argued that ethnic beliefs are best suited to help tribes relate to their world and to their place within it. According to this view, Christianity is a foreign religion less suited to their needs. We reject this view entirely. The gospel, which is acultural, transcends all cultures and is instantly applicable in any culture. The gospel is true in the universal sense, as opposed to the ethnic or localised sense. It is the birthright of every man to hear the gospel of our Lord Jesus Christ. The Bible teaches that the gospel is true for all, and is to be preached in all the world to every creature (Mark 16:15). The Lord Jesus tasted death for every man (Heb 2:9); gave Himself a ransom for all (1 Tim 2:6); and became a propitiation for the sins of the whole world (1 John 2:2). Further, all men everywhere are commanded to repent (Acts 17:30), and all are invited to come to Christ (John 7:37). God's attitude toward the world is best summed up in John 3:16: "For God so loved the world, that he gave his only begotten Son, that whosoever believeth in him should not perish, but have everlasting life."

Pluralist or Exclusive?

The gospel message is also true in the exclusive sense, as opposed to the pluralist sense. Postmodernism claims that all religious belief systems are saying the same thing, and that there is no religion that is true to the exclusion of all the others. The English philosopher John Hick (b.1922) is a leading representative of the pluralist approach. According to Hick, religions "constitute different 'lenses' through which the divine Reality is differently perceived."[57] Hick dismisses the exclusive claims of Christianity as being like the old earth-centred view of the universe, and compares the new theology of religions to the modern heliocentric view of the universe, "In the theology of religions a comparably simpler and more realistic model is today available in the theocentric or, better, Reality-centred, conception with its pluralistic implications. Here the religious universe centres upon the divine Reality; and Christianity is seen as one of a number of worlds of faith which circle around and reflect that Reality."[58]

That is utterly false. You cannot have the personal transcendent God of the Bible co-existing with the impersonal pantheistic god of Eastern mysticism. We contend that the relativistic/pluralistic approach is self-contradictory, illogical, and blasphemous. The Bible clearly states that there is no other God: "Assemble yourselves and come; draw near together, ye that are escaped of the nations: they have no knowledge that set up the wood of their graven image, and pray unto a god that cannot save. Tell ye, and bring them near; yea, let them take counsel together: who hath declared this from ancient time?

---

[57] Hick, John "Complementary Pluralism" in *The Christian Theology Reader* Ed. Alister E. McGrath (Blackwell Publishers, Oxford, 1955) p.335.

[58] Hick, John "Problems of Religious Pluralism" in *A Cloud of Witnesses - Readings in the History of Western Christianity* Ed. Joel F. Harrington (Houghton Mifflin Company, Boston, 2001) p.528.

who hath told it from that time? have not I the LORD? and there is no God else beside me; a just God and a Saviour; there is none beside me. Look unto me, and be ye saved, all the ends of the earth: for I am God, and there is none else" (Isaiah 45:20-22).

We must preach and teach that Jesus Christ is the only Saviour of sinners. There is no other Saviour. I suspect that it is on this issue of pluralism that many Christians sometimes feel under pressure. It is common to hear objectors say such things as "So you Christians are the only ones who are right, and everyone else in the world is wrong. I've never heard anything so arrogant!" It is easy to feel wrong-footed when someone accuses you in this way. However, no one else ever died for my sins and rose again to save me. The gurus, holy men, philosophers, and religious leaders of this world, can do nothing to remove my sin. Man's problem is not his ignorance, but his sin. Salvation is not in self-discovery or self-effort, but in "redemption through his blood, even the forgiveness of sins" (Col 1:14). It is the Bible alone which gives the correct diagnosis of human need, and gives the only remedy. This is good news, and we must tell it to all. It is not simply that the gospel is a better way, among many ways. Rather, there is no other way to God, no other gospel, and no other doctrine.

Fragmented or Unified?

The postmodernist, with his rejection of universal truths and objective knowledge, predicts that all human world-views (described by Lyotard as 'metanarratives') inevitably end in fragmentation. In other words, there is a gradual disintegration of political stability, social organisation, and the unified self. This conclusion would indeed be valid if God did not exist. The writer of Ecclesiastes understood that very well. If we leave God out of our thinking, we will eventually end up as fragmented people living in a fragmented society. Man was created as a unified being, capable of intelligent and loving fellowship with his Creator. Something has gone badly wrong. It is sin and guilt that are at the root of the problem. Alienation from God has ruined man and deconstructed him into something fragmented and lost. But happily there is a remedy. The gracious challenge of the Lord Jesus still echoes down to the men and women of our own generation: "Wilt thou be made whole?" (John 5:6). The wholeness that salvation brings is the subject of Paul's prayer for the Thessalonians: "And the very God of peace sanctify you wholly; and I pray God your whole spirit and soul and body be preserved blameless unto the coming of our Lord Jesus Christ" (1 Thess 5:23).

We know from our Bible that God controls history. Just as in ancient times all history led to the first coming of Christ into this world, so now all events are leading up to His second coming. The efforts of God-estranged men, culminating in the antichrist and his rebellion, will end in fragmentation and judgement. God Himself, at the second coming of Christ, will intervene in human history and unite a redeemed and transfigured creation under His Son. Paul wrote that God, in the fullness of time, would "gather together in one all things in Christ, both which are in heaven, and which are on earth; even in him" (Eph 1:10).

Conclusion

The philosophical movement of the late twentieth century, known as postmodernism, has produced a society that is increasingly rejecting the concepts of truth, purpose, and meaning. The postmodernist denies the existence of a personal God. He either attributes the phenomenon of life to blind, random processes, or he gives the credit to an intelligent but impersonal force within the universe. A typical postmodern man will be either atheistic or pantheistic. Not much has changed since Paul spoke at Athens to the Epicureans and the Stoics. We have noted earlier that the Epicureans took an atheistic/mechanistic world-view, while the Stoics took an animistic/pantheistic world-view.

We can discern these two ancient views represented in the books of today's popular science writers. Prevailing theories about science and cosmology eventually affect the thinking of the philosophers and the theologians. There are those who take the view that all life can be accounted for by random processes and non-purposive evolution. This Epicurean position is fiercely promoted today by Richard Dawkins, who holds the Chair for the Public Understanding of Science at Oxford University. He is the author of several best selling books, including *The Selfish Gene* and *The Blind Watchmaker*. Many undecided students have gone to university, only to be overwhelmed by Dawkins' popular defence of Darwinism. He is an avowed opponent of Christianity. The eighteenth century theologian, William Paley, had famously argued that you couldn't have a watch without a watchmaker. Paley applied the analogy to prove that you cannot have something as complex as an eye without a Designer. Paley, of course, was absolutely right! Dawkins rejects Paley's argument for intelligent design, and instead makes random evolution his god. Dawkins explains: "Natural selection, the blind, unconscious, automatic process which Darwin discovered, and which we know is the explanation for the existence and apparent purposeful form of all life, has no purpose in mind. It has no mind and no mind's eye. It does not plan for the future. It has no vision, no foresight, no sight at all. If it can be said to play the role of watchmaker in nature, it is the *blind* watchmaker."[59] Dawkins' ideas are not new, but are very firmly within the ancient camp of the Epicureans. He worships at the altar of blind evolution. The psalmist, by contrast, is in no doubt about the origin of complex organs: "He that planteth the ear, shall he not hear? he that formed the eye, shall he not see?" (Psalm 94:9).

On the other hand, there are scientists who acknowledge that the universe and biological life on earth have all the hallmarks of intelligent design. One such writer is Paul Davies, Professor of Mathematical Physics at the University of Adelaide, who claims that "science offers a surer path to God than religion."[60]

---

[59] Dawkins, Richard *The Blind Watchmaker* (Penguin Books, London, Repr. 1991) p.5.
[60] Davies, Paul *God and the New Physics* (Penguin Books, London, 1990) p.ix.

Davies, who has written numerous best selling books such as *The Mind of God* and *God and the New Physics*, freely argues for the concept of design as opposed to blind chance. However, Davies does not believe in the transcendent, personal God of the Bible. Rejecting the possibility of miracles, except the miracle of nature itself, Davies proposes a scientific understanding of the universe in which the emergence of life and consciousness is seen, not as a freak set of events, but fundamental to its lawlike workings. In other words, Davies has made the laws of physics to be his god. Davies, differing from the Stoics in terminology only, attributes life to the "lawfulness" of the cosmos. The explanation of Davies is a very old one. According to this view, the universe is self-organising in accordance with its own laws. Davies has more in common with the Stoics than he possibly realises. Similarly, the famous theoretical physicist and cosmologist, Stephen Hawkins, has written that the ultimate triumph of human reason will be the discovery of a complete and unified theory of everything. When we have such knowledge, according to Hawkins, "we will know the mind of God."[61]

Scientists are puzzled and perplexed that the universe appears to have been designed for life. The nuclear, gravitational and electromagnetic forces all have constants within very narrow limits that are exactly right for the existence of life. Why should this be? The scientists have offered an explanation known as the Anthropic Principle. This idea states that in the universe there exist regions where life can exist. It is claimed that we perceive the universe as being 'designed', simply because we exist, and if it had been different, we would not have been here to observe it. Therefore, according to this view, there is no "need" for God. Unbelievably, many scientists find this reasoning quite satisfying. For lesser mortals like ourselves, it would be very easy to miss the point! Frankly, the so-called Anthropic Principle is not an insight into the nature of the universe, but is a disingenuous piece of circular reasoning.

---

[61] Hawkins, Stephen W. *A Brief History of Time* (Bantam Press, London, 1988) p.175.

The Bible, on the other hand, tells us why the earth has been tailor-made for human life. Isaiah has given us the key: "For thus saith the LORD that created the heavens; God himself that formed the earth and made it; he hath established it, he created it not in vain, *he formed it to be inhabited*: I am the LORD; and there is none else (Isaiah 45:18).

For the last forty years the organisation known as SETI (Search for Extraterrestrial Intelligence) has been scanning the skies with religious zeal to find signs of life in outer space. The USA space programme is spending billions of dollars to find microbes[62] on Mars. Universities are introducing the new subject of Astrobiology. We are being told that a new "cosmotheology" will place human spirituality in a full cosmotheological and astrobiological context. Stephen Dick,[63] a science historian at the U.S. Naval Observatory, proposes abandoning the transcendent God of monotheistic religion in favour of what he calls a "natural God"- a superbeing located within the universe and within nature. Dick claims "With due respect for present religious traditions whose history stretches back nearly four millennia, the natural God of cosmic evolution and the biological universe, not the supernatural God of the ancient Near East, may be the God of the next millennium."

Should the believer be alarmed at the new scientific assaults on Christianity? Has science at last disproved the Bible? Not in the least! Firstly, we should remember that belief in extraterrestrial evolutionary life is not science, but pseudo-science. There is not a shred of evidence to support it. Secondly, the idea of a natural God within the universe is not new, but is simply the latest twenty-first century version of Stoicism.

---

[62] If traces of life are found on Mars, they may have come from comets and asteroids launched from Earth. See *In the Beginning: Compelling Evidence for Creation and the Flood* (7th Edition) by Dr. Walt Brown (Centre for Scientific Creation, 1995-2004) p.211.
[http://www.creationscience.com/onlinebook/LifeSciences15.html]
[63] Cited in Davies, Paul "E.T. and God" in *The Atlantic Monthly*, Sept 2003, Vol 292, Nr 2, 112-118.

The Christian student, and indeed the Christian parent, will increasingly have to defend the truth of the gospel against these kinds of objections from the world of science. How then are we to defend the truth of Christianity against such antagonistic "scientific" theories? The answer to this question is to be found in the Bible. The apostle Paul had to contend with very similar objections from the Greeks, who considered the gospel to be foolishness.

Our first answer must be that it is God who is the truth and reality behind this universe. When we speak of God, we are not using another name for nature, or physics, or evolution. We are speaking of the living, personal, transcendent God of the Bible who has created the universe, and has made Himself known in His Son, Jesus Christ. To God is ascribed the glory for creation in that great heavenly scene described by John: "Thou art worthy, O Lord, to receive glory and honour and power: for thou hast created all things, and for thy pleasure they are and were created" (Rev 4:11). It is not that God created the universe and then forgot about it. The role of Creator and Sustainer is also ascribed to the Son: "For by him were all things created, that are in heaven, and that are in earth, visible and invisible, whether they be thrones, or dominions, or principalities, or powers: all things were created by him, and for him: and he is before all things, and by him all things *consist*" (Col 1:16-17).

God created a perfect, working universe, which He shared with His creatures. When sin came into the world by way of man's disobedience, man became a dysfunctional, fragmented, alienated being. He was separated from God by whom, and for whom, he had been made. It was not as if man was merely dysfunctional and could be cured by some kind of corrective therapy - it was much more serious than that! He was actually a guilty sinner under sentence of death. The Lord Jesus provided salvation and redemption by offering Himself a sacrifice for sins on the cross. The problem of evil has been fully and forever addressed. On a future day, sin will be eradicated entirely from God's universe. The gospel restores and brings purpose and meaning to life, which had been lost in Eden. Further, salvation also brings *eternal* purpose and meaning. Paul told the Ephesian believers that God "hath raised us up together, and made us sit together in heavenly places in Christ Jesus: that in the ages to come he might shew the exceeding riches of his grace in his kindness toward us through Christ Jesus" (Eph 2:6-7).

The pantheistic notion is that men go through a cycle of reincarnations until finally they lose their self-identity, and are absorbed into the impersonal world soul. What a travesty of truth! On the other hand, the atheist believes that the entire universe, including time, matter and space, will end forever in a "big crunch." Either way, there is no future for the human body as such. By contrast, the Bible teaches that the believer is raised from the dead in an incorruptible, glorified, spiritual body (1 Cor 15:44). Further, the believer in eternity will be conformed to the image of God's Son (Rom 8:29), and will ever drink freely of the fountain of the water of life (Rev 21:6). Nothing will ever separate us from the love of God in Christ Jesus our Lord (Rom 8:39). The whole of creation, whether in heaven, or on earth, or under the earth, or in the sea, will then proclaim, "Jesus Christ is Lord, to the glory of God the Father" (Phil 2:11).

As we come to the end of our study, we conclude that postmodernism is not only an enormous lie, but is a violation of reason itself. The postmodern idea of relativism is a rejection of the concept of truth. This becomes a self-contradicting absurdity. Relativism in turn leads to pluralism, the notion that no religious proposition can be true in any exclusive or absolute sense. In other words, we cannot know anything for certain, because there isn't anything to know. Little wonder postmodern men believe that they have arrived at the end of philosophy. Postmodern thinking is the living proof of Paul's assertion that when men refuse to acknowledge God, they become fools. There are atheists who, like the Epicureans of old, deny the existence of God. We contend that it is a mistake of monumental foolishness to attribute the origin of the universe and consciousness to blind random processes. There are also pantheists who, like the Stoics of old, reject the personal, transcendent God of the Bible, and believe in a self-organising universe. This foolish doctrine leads to the worship of the creation rather than the Creator, and to the self-deification of man. Paul warns us about the danger of human philosophy contaminating our thinking about Christ: "Beware lest any man spoil you through philosophy and vain deceit, after the tradition of men, after the rudiments of the world, and not after Christ. For in him dwelleth all the fulness of the Godhead bodily" (Col 2:8).

In glorious contrast to human philosophy, be it Greek, modern, or postmodern, the Bible tells us about the true, eternal, living, triune, and personal God, who is the maker of heaven and earth. God made us with the purpose that we might know Him, serve Him, worship Him, enjoy Him, and love Him. God has spoken in the Person of His Son, our Lord Jesus Christ. It was at the cross that God dealt with the problem of evil and sin. Because of the death of the Lord Jesus on Calvary, God is able and willing to forgive sinners. Alienated, fragmented, guilty men can be reconciled to God, and made whole. We have the privilege to tell our postmodern friends that there are such things as truth, meaning and purpose. However, they are found in Christ alone. As long as we are in our sins, we will be alienated from the life of God, without meaning, purpose or hope in our lives. Without God, man is truly lost. When a sinner turns by faith to Christ for forgiveness and salvation, he is brought into a holy, loving, fellowship with God. Salvation brings meaning and purpose to our existence, not only for this life, but also in the eternal sense. We recall again the words of the Saviour: "I am the way, the truth, and the life: no man cometh unto the Father, but by me" (John 14:6). We point our readers to the Lord Jesus Christ, who is the truth and reality behind the existence of all created things, and who is the Saviour of sinners. Men are lost, and need to know the way. Men are deceived, and need to know the truth. Men are dead, and need life. We quote one more time the great gospel truth that Paul taught:

"For the Jews require a sign, and the Greeks seek after wisdom: but we preach Christ crucified, unto the Jews a stumbling block, and unto the Greeks foolishness; but unto them which are called, both Jews and Greeks, Christ the power of God, and the wisdom of God" (1 Cor 1:22-24).

Paul's message to the first century men of Athens is still God's ultimatum to twenty-first century men: "And the times of this ignorance God winked at; but now commandeth all men everywhere to repent: because he hath appointed a day, in the which he will judge the world in righteousness by that man whom he hath ordained; whereof he hath given assurance unto all men, in that he hath raised him from the dead" (Acts 17:30-31). May God help us to serve our generation by faithfully preaching and teaching the gospel of truth. We need to proclaim the *true* God, and teach what the Bible says about creation, sin, salvation, judgement, and eternity. We must emphasise that the Bible is true, not in a relative or culturally conditioned sense, but in the absolute, eternal, universal and objective sense. We can be *absolutely* certain of this assertion because God, who spoke in former times by the prophets, has in these last days spoken to us in His Son (Heb 1:1). With wondering and worshiping hearts, we recall the true and faithful words of our Lord Jesus Christ: "I am Alpha and Omega, the beginning and the end, the first and the last" (Rev 22:13). We must preach no other message save "Jesus Christ, and him crucified" (1 Cor 2:2). It will never be a popular message, because it puts all men in the wrong, condemning them as guilty sinners who need to be saved. The gospel is still the power of God for salvation to everyone who believes. It is a simple yet glorious truth to grasp for oneself that "Jesus died for me." There is no other way, no other Saviour, and no other doctrine.

We close this book with a glorious affirmation of truth, not in a relative or subjective sense, but in the absolute, eternal and universal sense: "Worthy is the Lamb that was slain to receive power, and riches, and wisdom, and strength, and honour, and glory, and blessing. And every creature which is in heaven, and on the earth, and under the earth, and such as are in the sea, and all that are in them, heard I saying, Blessing, and honour, and glory, and power, be unto him that sitteth upon the throne, and unto the Lamb for ever and ever" (Rev 5:12-13).

Bibliography

Textual Criticism

Anderson, Sir Robert *The Bible and Modern Criticism* (Pickering & Inglis, London and Glasgow, 7th edition, undated)

Anderson, Sir Robert *Daniel in the Critics' Den* (James Nisbet & Co, London, 1902)

Bruce, F.F. *The New Testament Documents - Are they reliable?* (William B. Eerdmans, Mich. 1983)

Bruce, F.F. *The Books and the Parchments - How we got our English Bible* (Pickering & Inglis, UK, 1984)

McDowell, Josh *The New Evidence that Demands a Verdict* (Thomas Nelson Publishers, Nashville, 1999)

Showers, Renald E. *The Foundations of the Faith - the revealed and personal Word of God* (Friends of Israel Gospel Ministry Inc., 2002)

Thomas, Robert L. *Evangelical Hermeneutics - The new versus the old* (Kregel, 2002)

Urquhart, John *The Inspiration and Accuracy of the Holy Scriptures* (Pickering & Inglis, undated)

Ancient, Modern and Postmodern Philosophy, and Christian Apologetics

Blanchard, John *Does God Believe in Atheists?* (Evangelical Press, Darlington, England, 2000)

Brown, Colin *Philosophy and the Christian Faith* (Inter-varsity Press, London, Reprint 1974)

Carson, D.A. *The Gagging of God - Christianity confronts pluralism* (Apollos, IVP, Leicester, England, 1996)

Dockery, David S. (Editor) *The Challenge of Postmodernism - an evangelical engagement* (BridgePoint Books, Victor Books, USA, 1995)

Geisler, Norman L. *Baker Encyclopedia of Christian Apologetics* (Baker Books, Grand Rapids, 1999)

Gooding, David *Christian Answer to Pagan Philosophies* (Tape Series recorded by Uplook Ministries, Grand Rapids, MI, 1997)

Gooding, David & Lennox, John *The Definition of Christianity - Distinguishing the essence of the Christian message from the confusion of Christendom* (Gospel Folio Press, MI, 1992)

Grenz, Stanely J. *A Primer on Postmodernism* (Wm. B. Eerdmans Publishing Co, Grand Rapids, 1995)

McGrath, Alister *The Twilight of Atheism* (Rider, London, 2004)

Penfold, Michael J, *Postmodernism* (Booklet published by Penfold Book & Bible House Ltd, Oxon, 2003)

Schaeffer, Francis A. *The Complete Works of Francis A. Schaeffer Volume 1 A Christian View of Philosophy and Culture* including "The God Who Is There" (1968), "Escape From Reason" (1968), "He Is There and He Is Not Silent" (1972), "Back To Freedom and Dignity" (1972), (Crossway Books, Illinois, 1982)

Silva, John W De *My Lord and My God - The Deity of Christ, The Perfect Man* (John Ritchie Ltd, Kilmarnock, Scotland, 2003)

Sire, James W. *The Universe Next Door - A guide to world views* (Inter-Varsity Press, England, 1988)

Veith, Gene Edward *Guide to Contemporary Culture* (Crossway Books, Leicester, 1994)

Zecharias, Ravi *Jesus Among Other Gods - The absolute claims of the Christian message* (Word Publishing, Nashville, 2000)

Zecharias, Ravi *Can Man Live Without God?* (Word Publishing Group, Tennessee, 1984)

Origins

Abou-Rahme, Dr Farid *And God Said... Science confirms the authority of the Bible* (John Ritchie Ltd, Kilmarnock, 1997)

Behe, Michael J. *Darwin's Black Box - The biochemical challenge to evolution* (Touchstone, NY, 1996)

Gish, Duane T. *Evolution - The fossils still say no!* (Institute for Creation Research, Cal. 1995)

Humphries, D.Russell *Starlight and Time - Solving the puzzle of distant starlight in a young universe* (Master Books, AR, USA, seventh printing 2002).

Macbeth, Norman *Darwin Retried* (Garnstone Press, London, 1974)

Morris, Henry M. & Parker, Gary E. *What is Creation Science?* (Master Books, CA 1987)

Peterson, Dennis R. *Unlocking the Mysteries of Creation* (Master Books, CA, 2002)

Swift, David *Evolution under the Microscope - a scientific critique of the theory of evolution* (Leighton Academic Press, UK, 2002)

Whitcomb, John C. & DeYoung, Donald B. *The Moon - Its creation, form and significance* (Baker Book House, Grand Rapids, Michigan, 1978)

Whitcomb, John C. & Morris, Henry M. *The Genesis Flood - The Biblical record and its scientific implications* (P&R Publishing Company, NJ, 42nd printing 1998)

New Age

Ankerberg, John & Weldon, John *Encyclopedia of New Age Beliefs* (Harvest House Publishers, Oregon, 1996)

Groothuis, Douglas R. *Unmasking the New Age* (InterVarsity Press, Illinois, 1986)

Hawkins, Craig S. *Goddess Worship, Witchcraft and Neo-Paganism* (Zondervan, USA, 1998)